Web Site Design

WITH THE

Patron in Mind

A STEP-BY-STEP GUIDE
FOR LIBRARIES

Susanna Davidsen
and
Everyl Yankee

AMERICAN LIBRARY ASSOCIATION

CHICAGO   2004

Design and composition by ALA Editions in Utopia and Verdana typefaces using QuarkXPress 5.0 for the PC

Printed on 50-pound white offset, a pH-natural stock and bound in 10-point cover stock by Victor Graphics

The paper used in this publication meets the minimum requirements of American National Standard for Information Sciences—Permanence of Paper for Printed Library Materials, ANSI Z39.48-1992. ∞

Library of Congress Cataloging-in-Publication Data
Davidsen, Susanna.
    Web site design with the patron in mind : a step-by-step guide for libraries /
Susanna Davidsen and Everyl Yankee.
        p.   cm.
    Includes bibliographical references and index.
    ISBN 0-8389-0869-1
    1. Library Web sites—Design.   I. Yankee, Everyl.   II. Title.
    Z674.75.W67D386 2004
    025.04–dc22   2003023148

Printed in the United States of America

08   07   06   05   04   5   4   3   2   1

To my husband Jack and sons John and Kit who put up with my absences and still provided unwavering support. And for my late Mom and Dad who went against family advice and sent me—a girl—to university despite it. (Sue)

To my husband Stan who put up with my continuous presence and still provided unwavering support. (Everyl)

And to librarians and library workers everywhere—in appreciation.

Contents

Acknowledgments

Thank you to Metta Lansdale and the Board of the Chelsea District Library of Chelsea, Michigan, for permission to use a photo of the McKune House.

Thank you to Cliff Haka and Faye Backie of the Michigan State University Library and Pete Cookingham of the Turfgrass Information Center at Michigan State University.

Thank you to Martha Geier for reading the manuscript and her encouragement and support.

And a special thank you to John Wylie for the graphics and his patience.

Foreword

By Karen G. Schneider

This book is a gift for all librarians who sense, deep down, that their libraries' web site needs a serious makeover but want to do it correctly from the ground up. In the firm but comfortable grip of authors Sue Davidsen and Everyl Yankee, you will learn that a web site exists first and foremost for its users—not to satisfy a designer's whim or to appease the maintainers' need for ease of use. As Sue and Everyl explain, there is no one user community, no single goal, no minute when you stick a fork in your web site and declare it done for good. Like any library service, to quote the great twentieth-century librarian S. R. Ranganathan, a web site is a "living organism."

Sue, a librarian, and her writing companion, Everyl Yankee, a usability specialist, are uniquely qualified to present the practical guidance you will find in these pages. A long time ago, when a 300-baud modem was something to brag about, Sue created the first virtual library on the Internet. Sue's model was so successful it was shamelessly copied by commercial portals such as Yahoo! and less shamelessly emulated by other librarians attempting to organize that vast information trash barge known as the Internet. It continues today as the Michigan eLibrary, nicknamed MeL, a sturdy, information-rich web portal popular with users throughout its home state.

Sue learned web usability by the seat of her pants, long before it became a glitzy catchphrase of the Internet boom. Or perhaps it's more accurate to say Sue *lived* web usability, because her essential librarian nature combined with her technical acumen made her acutely sensitive to every hurdle between the Internet and its many audiences. Without help from the gurus and pundits who would later flood the marketplace with literature (some of it quite good and some of it horrifyingly bad), she created methods and techniques to help users ford what usability experts call "the gulf of execution," those rough waters between the user's needs and the resources that will meet these needs.

Sue's recipe for success boiled down to another rule of Ranganathan's: "save the time of the reader." She experimented with an exciting concept, borrowed from library work: Internet information could be presented in organized chunks, arranged by subject. Thanks in large part to the work of such people as Sue, this hardly seems revolutionary today, but in 1992 most new Internet resources were shared by swapping emails, by postings to UseNet, and through small mailings, such as Scott Yanoff's weekly list of new Internet resources. When that crept up to three entire pages of new sites, we all began worrying about the vast boom of information ahead of us. Soon there might even be *thousands* of pages on the Internet! And here was MeL, offering sanctuary from chaos.

As new Internet technologies developed, the curse of "creeping featurism" arose. With the graphical Internet, every page had to be gussied up (and bogged down) with an enormous, slow-loading picture. The advent of animated graphics fostered a period in which many sites featured jittery graphics (and even the derisive phrase "jumping bologna" did not deter web page designers from creating pages that manically jittered and twinkled). Web sites have since groaned under the weight of irrelevant and unavoidable music, Javascript, pages that display best in this or that browser, or incomprehensible topologies designed around "advanced content management systems" that re-created the "information barge" experience at the micro-level. With the vast, collective unhinging of common sense known as the dot-com boom, it seemed at times that any web site, however mystifying and unnavigable, could attract millions of dollars of venture capital, if its creators wore the right shoes and glasses and attended the right parties.

Still, even in the pell-mell madness of the fin de siècle, MeL stayed true to its roots, every week providing more and more information, always getting a little easier to navigate, adding a splash of color now and then—not unlike a public library that periodically paints and renovates but makes sure its most comfortable chairs are in that patch of sun near the magazine section. Meanwhile, Sue worked several years at ProQuest, learning how to design databases that librarians would want to purchase, while her writing companion, Everyl Yankee, spent her time quietly practicing real usability work at the same company.

Around the time computers began to be available for ordinary people to buy, Everyl, an applied linguist by training and inclination, realized that language might actually become a two-way street, or even a technological highway for computer users. She decided to tackle in a practical way the fun, big problem of language and computers. She began by working at a university laboratory that made "talking computers"—wiring, repairing, observing, learning, and eventually becoming the "grease" to move the operation along as smoothly as possible.

What she saw was the necessity of the future. Computer technology's original early adapters—those whose physical or cognitive restrictions forced them to become adept with these new machines—were in turn forcing the engineers, therapists, and techies with whom they were teamed to understand that if these users could not use it, there was no point in trying. Courage and determination teamed with innovation to simplify the representation of the user's world by focusing on a pragmatic approach built from the everyday nouns we use for our most basic needs and wants.

Everyl continued to apply her understanding of how to represent the user's needs and worldview throughout the era of that unintentional red herring, the original and overly complicated graphical user interface, which monopolizes even today. She learned more and refined her ideas while consulting on web applications for the big companies. All this time she kept the simple ideas in front of her: keep an analytical approach; refine the design (or ditch the bad ones without remorse); acknowledge that users recognize and can use concrete interfaces; and, while juggling resources, always put the user first. Although there still is no speed lane for a computer user, interfaces can be better vehicles.

The library community can be grateful Sue and Everyl took the time to codify their knowledge in this book, and that they did it so well, in language that is as straightforward as the town pump. What will the future bring? I can't speak for the Web, but out in the real world, I see more users—and they are very lucky that librarians will have this book to help identify and meet their needs.

KAREN G. SCHNEIDER
Director, Librarians' Index
to the Internet, lii.org

ANOTHER BOOK ON WEB DESIGN?

If you've been in the technology section of a bookstore lately, you'll notice no shortage of web design books—web design for e-commerce, web design for fun and profit, web design for dummies. But here's one you probably didn't see: a web design book tailor-made for your library.

In this book, we'll teach you how to design a site for *your* users. An effective web site is one that allows a particular group of users to find the information they need quickly and effectively. Unfortunately, most books on web site design are more general. They provide little guidance on how to glean data about users and their habits and incorporate that data into the design. The methodology presented in this book provides step-by-step guidance on how to gather key information, distill it, and use it to build a practical, useful site for your patrons. The good news is that librarians already spend a great deal of time learning about their users. This knowledge, combined with a systematic approach that has its roots in usability, can be a powerful tool to create better library web sites.

Why is that important? A library's web site is no longer an add-on service but has become the library's presence to more and more users. In many campus communities, increasingly Internet-savvy young people spend little of their student life sitting in the library. As more adults become Internet users, the library web site becomes a convenient way to access the library's content and services. The central role of a library's web site places the importance of its design as high as the design of a circulation desk or a children's room.

Furthermore, a well-designed web site—one that's created for your users— is especially important considering the climate in which libraries now exist. Building projects are being put on hold and funding is being cut because of the well-traveled myth that "everything is on the Internet now." Librarians offer an organized entrée into the valuable content on the Internet as well as localized content and services. Your web site merges these two worlds into a convenient access point for your user. It is his or her work space while in your library's virtual space.

Another reason to focus on building a user-friendly web site now is to steer patrons toward quality information. Google and other web search engines promote an attitude that searching for information begins and ends with a single text-entry box. Libraries and their contents and services are overlooked even when the results are 12,000 documents of questionable content by questionable authorities. Too many users are learning that this is just the way the information world is. It isn't the way it should be, and library web sites can go a long way toward teaching users that targeted, quality information and help finding that information are available as conveniently as Google's search engine.

Making sure that a library's web site is convenient and provides the information and services that users expect and need in a way that users understand is paramount to providing the user with a good experience. A good experience translates into positive feelings toward the library, increased library (physical or virtual) usage, and increased support for the library in the user's community.

Usability is not a new concept to librarians. Services to the visually and physically impaired exist in most public libraries and in many academic libraries. The library community was one of the first to see the need of these users for information services. Usability is an extension of this concern. It's why library buildings are accessible as well as why we have such services as books on tape. Given that the World Wide Web is one more service that libraries provide, applying usability to it is another way to increase its accessibility.

A web site designed around usability does not need an overly flashy design. Libraries have little money to devote to web site building. Professional design firms are expensive, while your trustee's teenage son's best friend needs to be carefully supervised to keep your web site free of too many spinning, bouncing, flashing objects and copyrighted material that you have no rights to distribute. The methodology provided in this book can be used by a team or an individual to provide a usable working site for your library, whether it be academic, special, or public.

Examples in this book draw from all three types of libraries. We have tried to include examples that are unique to each type as well as those that cross the boundaries. Please forgive us if we left out something unique to your particular type of library. Special libraries by their very appellation tell us that they have some kind of unique quality. So while we may not have listed all of the objects that you may need, we teach you the process so you can design for your special library users.

Because most libraries already have a web site and will not be designing from scratch, we describe this process as if it were a redesign for your library site.

The process works equally well if you decide you are building from the beginning. Chapter 8 is devoted to helping you figure out how much redesign you need and how to apply the process. Some web sites are innately good sites and will need little in the way of fix ups, while others may be beyond saving and require that the designer or design team start over. We help you evaluate what state your current site is in and what you need to do to make it better.

Because librarians know so much about their users, you have a head start in the process. Many of the materials you will need to pull together will already exist or be in the combined heads of your staff and administrators. You may already have been doing some of the steps in our process without knowing it. Our methodology puts the steps into logical order and gives terminology to a library-specific version of this process. It will help you as the librarian, the designer, or both to focus your efforts on the important work you need to do, and it will save you steps and loops that can eat up your valuable time.

Our process combines the software development model with the librarian's mental model to create a way to systematically redesign your web site. This is orderly, creative problem solving that should prove fun and interesting to many librarians. If you would like in-depth information about the methodology from which it derives, please refer to the endnotes in chapters 3 and 7 as well as the bibliography, which may be of great interest to the technical folks on your team.

There are many checklists and grids throughout this book that will help you with the process.[1] Examples are taken from real-life libraries and their real-life users, problems, and web sites. We encourage you to make your own based on these.

How to use this book

In some ways, this book is like a cookbook—you'll assemble the ingredients, and we'll tell you what to do with them. There are too many variables, however, for us to offer you an exact recipe to follow. Everyone's patron groups are a little different—large public libraries differ from small ones as do college libraries and university libraries. Special libraries are even more diverse. When you've completed the steps in our process, you can use chapter 3 as a checklist for any new project you take on.

You don't need to be a web design specialist or information architect to use this book. We'll teach you what you need to know to create a usable, user-centered web site. For those of you who would like to learn more, we provide an extensive bibliography.

We follow a number of conventions in this book. Each chapter includes the purpose of the chapter, a redesign process chart when appropriate, a discussion of the chapter contents, and what to expect next. It also includes a chapter checklist.

We provide access to this book according to library roles, so the technical person who may be working with you could read chapters 1, 3, 4, 7, and 9. You may wish to discuss chapter 1 with your director as well as the section in chapter 5 on how to define targeted patron groups.

We don't use one library as a case study throughout the book because we're trying to cover the three major types of libraries. We do use the same public library, academic library, and special collections library (which we'll refer to as Turfgrass, a site we actually helped redesign) throughout, however, and interchange the types of libraries in the samples.

Information specific to the various types of libraries is indicated by the following icons:

Public Library

Academic
Library

Special
Library
(Turfgrass)

Terminology is explained throughout this book, but, for easy reference, we've included a glossary. We use the familiar concepts of "broaden" and "narrow" to help you complete your tasks in this process. This is the conceptual model, or metaphor, we use for the readers of this book. You'll learn more about conceptual models in chapter 4.

Things we wish we could cover

One area that we won't address in this book is the technical side of web site design. The underpinnings of the user interface change frequently with new standards and software releases, while the process we describe here has stood the test of time. If you work with a programmer, developer, or systems person, ask him or her to read this book to understand the process you're following. You'll have to step in when and if the technical person wants to design while he or she programs, which is not a good idea, as you will discover. We have provided in-depth technical resources about object-based design in the bibliography.

Other areas we aren't addressing in this book are:

Bread crumbs. We like these visual clues that tell the user where she or he is in a site, but you may not have the technological capability to do this.

Accessibility. We fully support efforts to make web sites accessible to individuals with disabilities. We've designed accessible web sites and interfaces, but the topic deserves more coverage than we can offer here.

Multiple languages. Our special-library example has multiple languages, but culture-based design considerations are beyond the scope of this book.

Children and teens as in-depth topics. The design principles and process we use work equally well for them when they are treated as a patron group, so we don't single out any special treatment for them. Jakob Nielsen covers special design issues for children. See the bibliography for the URL for his web site.

Visual design and graphics. You will most likely work with a graphic artist to make your site attractive and pleasing to use. The only advice we'll give you on this is don't use too many colors and don't have images that spin, whir, or blink. Remember, your web site is a marketing piece for your library and, like a brochure, should be attractive and professional. In the bibliography, you will find URLs to our design site and others.

Searching. Both authors have a great deal of experience designing search interfaces, but this is another subject that requires extensive treatment that is beyond this book's topic coverage.

Evaluation. We cover evaluating as the final step in the process, but other authors offer in-depth treatment of this topic in a library context. These sources are listed in the bibliography.

What we do cover

What is included? Here's a snapshot of what each chapter covers: Chapter 2, "Redesigning for Users—The Basics of Usability and User-Centered Design," discusses a current approach to designing web sites (and software applications, from which most of this stuff derives). Called user-centered design, it focuses on designing or redesigning by working directly from what patrons want from libraries. The history of user-centered design is briefly presented.

Chapter 3, "Redesigning—An Overview," introduces a timeline and answers the question "How do I get from idea to product?" at the overview level. You will learn that you will need to collect the following data for site redesign: your site goals, your targeted patron groups, and their specific behavior.

Chapter 4, "The Vision Thing—Goals for Your Web Site," discusses the need for a cohesive site goal, used initially to focus on these questions: Why are you creating a web site and for whom? Why is a mission important to a web site? What happens when you don't have a mission? How will you test whether your site has successfully fulfilled its mission? Sample vision statements are introduced and analyzed. The chapter contains information and exercises to help readers write a goals statement. Chapter 4 also introduces the conceptual model, a concept crucial for making sure that site builders are thinking like patrons.

Chapter 5, "Patrons—Who They Are," discusses in depth how to determine which patrons are crucial to the success of the elibrary and how to define them thoroughly. Implications for redesign are introduced.

Chapters 6 through 9 take you through the steps of understanding patron behavior, actual redesigning, evaluating, and refining the design.

Chapter 10 is a brief overview of evaluating your web site. For more in-depth reading on this topic, we refer you to the bibliography on page 109.

Now that we've laid the groundwork, let's get started on usability principles and practices.

NOTE

1. Some grids are derived from Hackos and Redish.

REDESIGNING FOR USERS
The Basics of Usability and User-Centered Design

2

This chapter introduces usability, provides definitions of it, and explains its history. The chapter also introduces the notion of user-centered design, which encompasses designing or redesigning by working directly from what patrons want from libraries.

At the end of this chapter, you will understand:

- the definition of usability
- the advantage of usability
- the downside of usability
- user-centered design
- the strengths of user-centered design
- some important usability principles
- how to redesign with usability

What is usability?

The most concise definition of usability we know is "fit for use."[1] Something that is useful has usability, in simple terms. If patrons come to your library and are able to use your services, then your library has usability. If they encounter difficulties or frustrations, then perhaps some of the "principles of usability" need to be applied.

What is the advantage of usability?

Usability professionals seek to make products easy to use and the people who use the products happy—or at least satisfied—that they decided to use them. Usability has traditionally evolved as a method to help increase productivity; however, we recognize that while some patrons coming to a library may be seeking to be productive by accomplishing their goals quickly, we also know that the pure pleasure of browsing is entertainment and certainly not productive in a traditional sense.

Having a clear-cut process to make a usable library site helps keep control of resources. An example of a process that makes your library usable by controlling resources is the process that results in getting books onto your shelves. First, you apply the accession process when you receive a book. Next, the book is cataloged and classified, and the bibliographic record is added to your catalog. The book is then labeled and shelved. A lack of any of these processes would result in a less usable library. A library's physical processes have been in place for many years. Web technology is still new enough that we're dealing with underdeveloped and competing processes or, as in this book, a process from another field adapted to the library world.

One benefit that supersedes productivity is a decreased amount of time for patrons to learn how to use something. A well-designed web site is easy to learn to use, and it is easy to use when the patron returns, despite the length of time between uses. In other words, if someone is an infrequent visitor to your library, it should take just a little time for that person to remember how to get around and find what she or he is seeking if your library is intuitive (something we'll define in chapter 8).

Another benefit of redesigning for usability is that a well-designed site is easy to change. There's a clear plan, and if something does not seem to be working well, there's a clear development process that can be reviewed and adjusted quickly and easily. Site maintenance that follows the design plan is also relatively quick because the site has a logic behind it that allows for both flexibility and expansion.

Perhaps the biggest advantage for the library will be patron satisfaction. Patron satisfaction depends on a number of variables, but it is essential to libraries in terms of support. The support might be in the form of tax dollars, successful fund-raising campaigns, increased budget allocations, or other support that translates into dollars. Or it may just be the goodwill and happiness of the community you serve. A more likely scenario is that both will prove to be worthwhile goals.

What is the downside of usability?

If there's a downside, we don't know what it is. Because *usability* has a broad definition and buzzword status, it sometimes becomes an empty concept. Bad usability—and it's rarely known as "un-usability"—generally comes from a vague or misguided approach to the design process. Often people think that usability is the same as screen design or what color or style font to use—and that becomes a downside because it's based on a vague approach to making a site work for users. Genuine usability suffers the ill effects.

A word about graphic artists and usability—few usability professionals are screen designers. Most are focused on analysis—determining user behavior (the basis for good usability), or testing or evaluating products for usability, or both. A few rare ones have both usability analysis and design training and can provide direction and help throughout the process, but this is hardly necessary for success. Any team with strong resources can learn about usability and develop a fine web library together.

What is user-centered design?

Sometimes user-centered design is also called human-centered design. Both these phrases give the crucial clue: if your web site reflects the way users, not the staff, think about and use the library, then it's user centered. Designing something for people to use is very simple, yet extremely hard to do—and often it's very difficult to do because we, the designers, already know either how to best use something or the quickest way to do something. Computer programs, which of course are the underlying systems in our online libraries, are efficient, and people are not efficient—in fact, they are kind of messy or sloppy in how they do things. They forget pieces of what they are doing or who wrote something they want to look up, but they remember that "the guy lived in Italy in the eighteenth century" or "she was a basketball player who married that movie star" or other not clearly "indexable" and retrievable bits of information.

How did user-centered design evolve?

User centered is the opposite of system centered. Historically, computers were for technical people who didn't worry much about an interface or an easy way to perform their work because the computer was used for technical work. Toggle switches, punch cards, and all kinds of esoteric ways to put data into a computer and retrieve them were the standard, not to mention the nearly indecipherable language programmers used to perform their tasks. Some of that language still seeps out onto the screen in the form of strange sentences in error messages, code snippets on 404 screens, and so on.

As computers became more common, people who weren't so esoterically interested in only the technical side of the machine began to use them. Both text-based (menu-driven) as well as graphical interfaces began to be used. However, the techies who were used to interacting with computers in a complicated way were also the people who were building the interfaces. Note that we are not saying "designing" but, rather, "building." The history of the computer interface was historically dominated by the software—or even the hardware—engineer.

Boring as this sounds, the repercussion is even worse than the reciting. To make this explanation short, let's just jump back to the definition of *system centered*—the idea that an interface reflects the mind-set of the person who makes it and who is looking at how the computer is working from the inside out, or system side out.

Somewhere along the way, software programmers realized the potential of the computer as a widespread tool for nonprogrammers and began to work on the idea of user-friendly interfaces for the machine (although the term *user friendly* wasn't invented yet). However, since the luxury (or necessity) of working with a nontechnical user was novel, inefficient, and expensive, a user-friendly interface rarely became a reality.

As computers became increasingly cheaper and more common, consumers demanded that the computer be easier to use. After all, it's supposed to be a tool, and the best tools are those that are easiest to use. (If this seems oversimplified, it is, but think of an automobile as a tool—it's not extremely simple, yet the best functional designs in cars are those that are easiest to drive and that reflect the increasing use of vehicles by nonengineers.)

Meanwhile, the system-centered approach is always with us. It's evident when a software or web program or web site is difficult to use, and why is that? One reason is that the program reflects the way the machine needs to work to make the program function. And why should we, the users of the computer, care about that? It's a lot like someone requiring you to understand the history of the internal combustion engine when all you want to do is drive the car to the grocery store. Any good design of a complex thing hides the complexity so that people using it can do so without any heavy intellectual engagement.

The second reason a web site is difficult to use, and perhaps the most important reason for us, is that many times the computer software or web application reflects the way that the person who programmed it thinks, not the way that the person who will use it thinks. This may be because the programmer is very far removed from the actual users and has to make up what he or she thinks they would do rather than base the design on any actual contact with users.

Remember, if the program reflects the way the person who will use it thinks, then it's not system centered but user centered.

We're just librarians.
Is it important to know this?

Knowing the difference between user centered and system centered is important for two reasons. First, it's very easy to design from the system-centered approach, and, in fact, you will probably do it naturally. The web application development staff as well as the librarians on your team may find it very difficult to stop thinking in this way. (It's natural to think from a practical viewpoint: "Hey, I don't know what they'd do, so I'll just do it the easiest, slickest, etc., way," or "I bet they'd do *x* and *y* and that's how I'll proceed.") And we're speaking from personal experience!

Second, to design for users, you always have to look in the same direction the users are looking and represent their viewpoint. How do we accurately represent patrons' viewpoints? This is called using a conceptual model, and we'll discuss it in detail in chapter 4. The conceptual model will be the blueprint for the library web site, and it provides the following redesign guidelines for you:

1. It keeps you on track because you have to either follow the model or obtain a consensus when changing the model.
2. It saves resources because you can decide what a change will cost you, whether it's worth it, and whether you have enough time to make the change.
3. It provides a model for programmers so that they work from the patron's perspective and don't second-guess the way a patron would think.

What are usability principles?

One of the classic definitions of *usability* is that it is measured by "the extent to which a product can be used by specified users to achieve specified goals with effectiveness, efficiency and satisfaction in a specified context of use."[2] Breaking this down, *effectiveness* for us means "how well patrons can achieve a goal." *Efficiency* means "how difficult it is for patrons to achieve a goal," and *satisfaction* means "how comfortable and accepting patrons are with their results."

As we go through the process of redesign, you may be thinking that some of these criteria can't be measured very exactly or perhaps don't apply to some of the things patrons do at a library. This is true. In preparing usability assessments, evaluations, or tests, sometimes the effort may exceed the benefits. In chapter 9, we'll talk about how to measure usability by using these principles as well as by using the goals we've set for the online library along the way.

Along the way, *learnability* has been added to the usability definition just noted. In our context, it means "how easy it is for patrons to learn how to achieve their goals." It also means how easy it is for patrons to pick up where they left off if they have previously used the library site. In other words, they do not have to completely relearn every time, even if they use the site infrequently.

For some years, usability experts have adhered to a set of ten principles developed by usability guru Jakob Nielsen[3] (see bibliography). These principles are often called *heuristics* (or rules of thumb), and many of them are going to directly apply to our redesign. We are going to paraphrase them here to apply to usability for our library patrons (the original principles are incorporated within this list).

1. Never let the patron become lost in the library (unless he or she wants to!).
2. Make the online library mirror aspects of a physical library so patrons have their own, familar, clear metaphor of the library as guidance.
3. Be sure that the patron can do whatever she or he expects to be able to do, or should be able to do, at any time.
4. Keep things consistent in the library so patrons will know what to expect. And make sure patrons know what you are talking about.
5. Don't make it easy for patrons to make common mistakes.
6. Make surroundings and items in the library familiar and clearly displayed so patrons can use what they see to navigate as well as to accomplish their goals.
7. Make it easy for patrons to change their minds or to be able to do something else. Provide shortcuts for the patron "pros."
8. Keep things simple and pleasing for patrons so they're not overwhelmed and so their experience will be pleasant.
9. Help patrons to easily recover from a mistake and continue to achieve their goal by defining problems and recommending solutions.
10. Provide help in every way possible for patrons, even though you've designed the library so that patrons should not require help!

Several new guidelines have been developed and added to this list by OCLC since Nielsen first proposed these principles.[4] They are (in our own paraphrasing):

11. Make it obvious to patrons how things work in the library.
12. Don't overwhelm patrons with too much information about how to do something.
13. Let patrons discover at their own pace.
14. Don't promise patrons something you can't or won't deliver.

It's starting to sound like a mission or vision statement, isn't it? That's encouraging. Many of the pieces you may need for this redesign process are already available for you to use.

How do we redesign with usability?

Now we're ready to go. We've learned about usability and a little about user-centered design. We understand the difference between a system orientation or viewpoint and a user-centered viewpoint. Next, we are going to look at the process of redesigning in detail.

When you begin to redesign, you may encounter two major issues, and neither of them is about the process of redesign (which in itself is lengthy, but not difficult, to learn). One issue may come from those who are observing your redesigning and are not familiar either with the underlying principles of usability or with the process you are using. They may perceive you as wanting to tear the whole site down. Your redesigning, though, if it contains the strong set of analysis materials that we recommend that you prepare, can allow you to make quick, cheap, easy changes that will greatly improve site usability without a total teardown. (In fact, we will discuss exactly when, how, and how much to redesign in chapter 8, so don't be discouraged if you get this type of comment or criticism.)

The second issue that you may encounter arises because the redesign process, although easy to do, isn't quickly explained. While you are patiently working away at the framework needed for the redesign, someone else may be busily changing the site, often based on something he or she has seen and liked elsewhere without regard to any underlying usability principles or practices. Practicing usability and user-centered design is often perceived as a glamour job—it requires little effort and gives lots of reward, and anybody can do it. The design process can be likened to cataloging and classifying a book. Librarians know how much more is involved than just parking an architecture book on the shelf next to other architecture books. The process of cataloging, with all of its attention to hierarchies, painstaking descriptions, and terminologies, lies behind the ease of finding a book on the shelf. The reality usually includes lots of initial detail work and thinking about categorization, organization, and how tasks are actually done. Don't be discouraged!

What about design itself?

The concept of designing involves some principles that help to unify the site and make it "look right." Because we don't know what resources you have, we have included some information about how to design for user-friendly, intuitive sites in chapter 8, "Design or Redesign?"

What's next?

Chapter 3 introduces the entire process of user-centered design. Chapters 4 through 7 will take you step-by-step through one proven method of user-centered design that we have used successfully in redesigning library web sites.

Chapter 2 checklist

- What is going to define usability for *your* library site?
- What are the advantages and disadvantages of user-centered sites?
- What principles do you need to follow for your site?
- What caveats should you be aware of when redesigning for usability?
- What examples of usability and un-usability exist now within your library web site?

NOTES

1. *The American Heritage Dictionary of the English Language,* © 2000 by Houghton Mifflin Company, available at www.dictionary.com.
2. International Standards Organization, "Human-Centred Design Processes for Interactive Systems," *Report ISO 13407:1999* (Geneva, Switzerland: International Standards Organization, 1999).
3. Jakob Nielsen's original List of Ten Heuristics is available at http://www.useit.com/papers/heuristic/heuristic_list.html
4. OCLC's heuristics are listed at http://www.oclc.org/usability/heuristic/set.htm

REDESIGNING
An Overview

3

T his chapter provides you with an overview of how the redesign is accomplished and introduces a project timeline. It also introduces the redesign process chart and sets the stage for you to start working through the steps involved in redesign. *Note:* If you are planning to redesign, this chapter is probably the most important to read.

Redesigning a usable site is not complicated, but the process is lengthy and detailed. We're introducing a process chart to help you keep track (see fig 3-1). Once you have mastered the simple steps outlined in this chapter, you can apply them to anything that could benefit from usability. The process itself will be explained in detail throughout chapters 4 through 7. When you have worked through the examples and exercises in those chapters, you will have mastered the entire process thoroughly.

At the end of this chapter, you will understand:

- what redesigning is
- the process that gets you from idea to redesign
- what information you need to have
- when you should gather this information

PHASES			
Set Site Goals	Analyze Site	Redesign Site	Evaluate Site

FIGURE 3-1
Redesign Process Chart

- in what order you must do the steps in the process (organizing)
- what to do if you can't do all of this stuff

Note: Up to this point in the book we've discussed "users." Now, as we begin to apply process to the library world, we're going to talk about our very specific set of users, patrons.

What is redesigning?

Redesigning is defined as salvaging what you have and reusing it. It's all about how much you take apart and what level you need to tear down to before you completely start over. Cosmetic changes (improvements to the site's appearance only) are not redesign—in fact, they are steps backward in providing a site your patrons will use and like.

As you work through this book, you'll learn how much change your site will need by reviewing the underlying structure of the site and assessing how closely it adheres to the basic structure we're proposing. Then you'll know exactly what redesigning will be needed for your site.

What is the process that gets us from idea to redesign?

Redesign is mostly planning, discussing, and rearranging what you already have, with some additional work obtaining what you don't have but will need. As in many endeavors, most of the work of redesign is in the planning, not in the execution.

Should you design or redesign? There are advantages to redesigning. Because we have an existing site, with lots of items within it, we are going to use what we have. This makes the initial work of gathering information fairly easy because we can use what we already have. In fact, we may discover that much of the site has a kind of unity, but because the unifying principles we'll look at later are not clear to us as designers, we are off the mark slightly.

Redesigning comprises the following phases: analysis, redesign and implementation, and evaluation. The redesign process chart at the beginning of this chapter shows these phases and tasks.

Each phase will be introduced in its own chapter with examples and explanations and a process chart denoting the tasks for that phase. Note that you may skip any steps you like, but doing so may directly affect the usability value of the redesign and may cost additional resources later. We recommend that you read through the following brief overview of each phase to see which ones you will need.

THE ANALYSIS PHASE

As in most successful endeavors, there will be a great deal of information to collect and more than one attempt to make it right. Also as in successful endeavors, there will be more planning and analysis than would ever seem necessary.

There is much information to collect during the analysis phase. In usability work, we perform all this analysis for one reason: when it's time to evaluate, we may find that we are off center with our redesign in specific areas. We want to be able to quickly and easily correct our redesign. The materials we have collected during analysis will be invaluable for pinpointing what we have done wrong and helping us quickly correct it. Although analysis can become very tedious, rarely will we find that we have done too much up front!

We've broken out setting the library web site's goals from the analysis phase—it's often considered part of that phase—to emphasize the importance of this step. First, define and agree upon the library web site's goals. Then we collect all the information we have or need to learn about patrons, their objectives and goals, and how they typically perform their work. (We can also use this information about patrons' work habits to invent technological improvements to our site that patrons want.) Next, we need to clearly decide who we are serving. The people who come to the library may be a homogeneous group, as in a special collections library, or an extremely diverse group, as in a public library. All of these groups can be categorized and classified for analysis.

We discuss which groups of patrons are important to us and why, and we also make some difficult choices about which patron groups we cannot support at the level we would like. *Note:* Chapter 5, "Patrons—Who They Are," provides detailed information about how to do this. Chapter 6, "Tasks—Understanding What Patrons Want to Do," discusses specific patron behaviors it is important for you to understand.

When we've collected this information, we are ready to move on to the redesign phase.

THE REDESIGN PHASE

To redesign, we take all the pieces that we've collected and reassemble them into in our library web site so that it provides exactly what our newly defined patron groups expect from a visit to the library. *Note:* Chapter 9, "The Process of Redesigning," will discuss this in detail and take you through the process step-by-step.

Software programmers usually follow the redesign phase with the implementation phase, in which the application or web site is actually programmed. But we want to make a point here. We are incorporating the implementation phase into our redesign phase because nowadays user-centered redesign combines redesigning and programming in what are called *iterations*. That means that as often and as repeatedly as we can, we redesign something and then test it immediately with users to determine how well our redesign is user centered. At that point in the process, fixes are quick, cheap, and accurate. (Contrast this with system-centered applications, traditionally "thrown over the wall" for delivery and sometimes for usability testing. Problems that users encounter are generally very expensive and time consuming to fix and are often a low priority because the programmers have to move on to other projects.)

During the redesign phase, try to incorporate as many tests with patrons as you can to determine the accuracy of your redesign. Launch day is not the time to find out!

THE EVALUATION PHASE (SOME SAY TESTING)

The final phase in redesign is evaluation, or testing (see fig. 3-1). Volumes have been written about how to test for usability. Very briefly, usability best practices say that you should try as often as possible to have real patrons perform typical, real tasks, preferably for the first time, on the site and then determine how well the site allows them to do these tasks successfully. This is a very broad and not clearly measurable objective, but for reasons discussed later, it should serve your purpose quite well without using a lot of resources.

Please, for the least expensive and most efficient use of your resources, place this evaluation within your redesign phase. This will ensure that any significant changes your library web site will need can be made because you still have someone available to make them.

Chapter 10, "Evaluating and Testing," briefly discusses the basics of testing. By the way, we prefer to call this step evaluation rather than testing because an evaluation is generally not as rigid as a test and thus avoids confusion about how much we can really measure.

What information do we need to have for redesign?

Before beginning redesign, you must have some crucial information that will allow you to make informed decisions. The good news is that when this rather substantial analysis phase is finished, the redesign phase becomes self-evident, and accomplishing it becomes comparatively quick. The following sections detail the crucial information you need to collect.

Goals document from the mission or the vision statement

If you do not have a mission or vision statement, you will need to assemble or write one for the following reasons: (1) it will be a point of reference or provide clarification for site goals; (2) you will need a *goals document* to assure that the team stays focused on the original goals throughout this process; and (3) it will provide clear direction during the redesign process as to how prominently or where specific elements are placed within the web site. The goals will also help you decide how to measure the usability of the site.

Here's a tip: while it's tempting to skip this step or postpone it to the end, it's better to struggle through it because should you find yourself in a weighty discussion about how something within the site works, we assure you from experience that a decision will not come about quickly unless there is a goals statement to focus the discussion.

Information about your targeted patron groups

You will need to collect information about the people who use the library or in some way affect the success of the library. There are many potential services and much content that your library can provide, but it's important to focus both on the goals of your library and on the people who specifically fulfill the library's goals. Because we are going to classify these patrons by characteristics that make them similar, we call them patron groups. From a set of all patron groups, you'll decide exactly which patron groups to target with your library's services and content.

Information about your patron groups' specific behavior

After targeted patron groups have been determined, you will be mapping out exactly how patrons reach their goals and using this information to redesign your web site. We also call this *task analysis.*

Information about what patrons access or manipulate while reaching their goals

The final piece of information to collect will be all the items patrons actually handle when in a library to use throughout our newly redesigned user interface. These items are called *library objects* in the particular type of process that we are discussing throughout this book. (Now you know that you are going to be participating in *object-oriented interface design;* more about this method can be found in the bibliography.[1])

Redesigning

19

How do we organize the process?

The expanded redesign process chart in figure 3-2 illustrates the order in which these steps must occur. The top level (Set Site Goals, Analyze Site, Redesign Site, Evaluate Site) shows the timeline for your project. The level below shows tasks needed to be done—for example, under Set Site Goals, tasks would be to review the mission and vision statements.

PHASES and TASKS			
Set Site Goals	**Analyze Site**	**Redesign Site**	**Evaluate Site**
Review Mission and Vision	Define Patrons, Tasks, and Library Objects	Design Using Patrons and Tasks	Evaluate Site with Patrons

FIGURE 3-2
Expanded Redesign Process Chart

We highly recommend you start at the beginning and work through the process. Besides the obvious, this helps assure that your team will agree that your newly redesigned library web site accurately reflects the information you will be collecting.

What order should we do these things in?

Keep the order we propose. Needed first are mission/site goals and patron groups, then the specific behavior of patrons should be determined.

You may need to adjust your launch to fit an academic schedule (allowing sufficient time to alert faculty and staff about changes) or to fit around setting up training schedules, time for materials documentation, the founder's birthday, or any other important event.

Note that *when* you are evaluating the site will affect the schedule because of patron availability to test your redesign. If it's school break, for example, you may be short of evaluators. Remember, you may have to work backward from when you will have actual users available.

In chapter 5, "Patrons—Who They Are," the redesign schedule for the sample special collections library is built around the library board's scheduled meetings as well as special collections patrons' annual meetings. We introduce our web site changes during this time, adding some publicity into the launch. It is crucial to have patron support for our redesign because one of our library objectives is to obtain continuing support for the library through the financial gifts of happy patrons.

What if we can't do all of this stuff?

There is an extensive discussion about redesign in chapter 8; it is useful at any stage in this process because it discusses the types of redesigns typically undertaken for web sites. You might want to finish reading this chapter and, after understanding the overall concept that we present, read the chapter 8 discussion about how much redesign you'll need to do.

One of the examples in this book, Turfgrass, the special collections library, has been undergoing a redesign over several years and is still undergoing change. We did not have the resources to devote to a complete redesign when we started, and we still don't. In addition, with some of the patron groups we are targeting being resistant to change, we have made incremental changes where other redesign teams might work more quickly. (It's been an important objective to have complete user approval for our redesign.) So, you may be able to do much of the process but not very quickly.

Patrons are resistant to changes in a library redesign. Remember that a little change that's an improvement is much safer than a complete change, even if the complete change tests as a success before it's launched.

What's next?

Chapter 4 discusses how to use your vision and mission statements to create goals for your web site. If you don't have mission and vision statements, we'll remind you how to create them. We'll create a new document, the goals statement, as a basis for your goals document.

As you work through these chapters, you will collect the information needed for the analysis phase of the redesign. Actually, you will also complete a thorough review of your web site and determine about 85 percent of the type of redesigning you should do. Much of the redesign at this point is ready to put on paper, during your design phase.

Chapter 3 checklist

- How much redesigning might your site need?
- What are the steps in the redesign process?
- When should you gather the information you need?
- What might your tentative schedule for redesign be?

NOTE

1. Some of the ideas and concepts discussed in this book are based on IBM's OVID methodology, albeit presented in a very simplified way. See the bibliography and IBM's Ease of Use web site at http://www.ibm.com/easy for more information about this excellent resource. Developers especially will be interested in the in-depth methodology.

THE VISION THING
Goals for Your Web Site

4

All right, you're probably saying, "Please don't make me write another vision statement!" Don't panic. We don't want you to rewrite your vision and mission statements; we're just giving you another use for them. After all the time, money, sweat, and tears you invested, it's nice to be able to use them for a new purpose. Your vision and mission statements can help you create a better web site. If your library doesn't have vision and mission statements, you will need to create them or find something comparable.

At the end of this chapter, you will understand:

- what a vision statement is
- what a mission statement is
- how to identify possible patron groups and goals using the vision and mission statements
- how to write a goals statement for your web site
- what a conceptual model is

Mission, vision—why are they important?

One of the biggest mistakes that web site designers or design teams make is to lack a goal for their site. The site ends up aimlessly wandering through services and tasks, and you never know if you met any of your patrons' needs. Vision and mission statements can help you create a goals statement for your site (see fig. 4-1).

			PHASES and TASKS			
Set Site Goals		**Analyze Site**		**Redesign Site**	**Evaluate Site**	
Review Mission and Vision		Define Patrons, Tasks, and Library Objects		Design Using Patrons and Tasks	Evaluate Site with Patrons	

FIGURE 4-1
Redesign Process Chart—Mission and Vision

What's the difference between a vision and a mission?

Here's how the *Economist Business Encyclopedia Dictionary* distinguishes the two:

> *Mission statement:* . . . a short, memorable statement clarifying the reasons for the existence of an organization, and expressing what its purpose and long-term objectives are. A mission statement is similar to a vision statement.
>
> *Vision statement:* . . . a statement giving a broad, aspirational image of the future that an organization is aiming to achieve. Vision statements express corporate vision. They are related to mission statements, and there is much contradictory opinion about the differences or similarities between them. This debate is perhaps irrelevant to the process suggested by both, of describing an organization's road ahead.[1]

For many, the mission statement is the "why," as in "why are we here?" and the vision statement is the "how," as in "how do we get from here to there?" or "how do we know we're there?" The mission statement defines a purpose, and the vision statement defines a goal. But, as stated by the *Economist Business Encyclopedia Dictionary*, the differences are slight and open to much debate and opinion.

How do you develop a vision?

Review your vision statement with an eye toward how you want your web site to help you reach that vision. Here are some sample vision statements:

> A world of information and ideas within reach of every Calgarian.
> —*Calgary Public Library, Alberta, Canada*

> Each resident will enjoy satisfying lifelong learning and leisure experiences as a result of their contact with the Library, provided by a knowledgeable

staff and a sophisticated array of current materials, in sufficient quantity to satisfy local demand, complementing the offerings of other local recreational and educational institutions.

Glen Ellyn residents, from preschoolers to seniors, will be introduced to information technology in a manner appropriate to individual learning styles, enhancing their ability to utilize electronic resources for their individual benefit. —*Glen Ellyn Public Library, Glen Ellyn, Illinois*

Brooklyn Public Library will be a vital center of knowledge for all, accessible 24 hours a day, and will be a leader in traditional and innovative library services which reflect the diverse and dynamic spirit of the people of Brooklyn.
—*Brooklyn Public Library, Brooklyn, New York*

The Aquinas College Woodhouse Library envisions a future integrating technological advancements with traditional services.

The library views the challenges of a rapidly changing environment as an opportunity to build on its strengths and achievements, continuing to make it a center of the Aquinas learning community.
—*Aquinas College Library, Grand Rapids, Michigan*

It is IIT's vision to be among the leaders in the world in providing excellent teaching, research, services and innovative technology assisted instruction. The library will be a central part of the realization of this vision. Throughout the 21st century, the Paul V. Galvin Library and its branches will be recognized worldwide as a premier library in creating a new environment for excellence in the provision of instruction, collections, information services and technology. The library will expend every possible effort to communicate, and conserve knowledge in order to enrich the capacity of individuals to think, learn, act and lead. It will provide the university and its community with the most friendly physical space and experienced staff. The library staff will have the skills, flexibility and organizational support to keep pace with the rapidly changing environment; to apply new technologies to assist users; and to continuously improve and optimize the library's systems.
—*Paul V. Galvin Library at the Illinois Institute*
of Technology, Chicago, Illinois

Mississippi State University Libraries will continue to serve as the premier campus information resource by providing its communities of users an ongoing, creative, technologically advanced library program that supports, enhances and inspires education, scholarship and service of the highest caliber in an environment of free and open inquiry and with a commitment to excellence. —*Mississippi State University Library, Starkville, Mississippi*

To stimulate the economy and help individuals statewide by developing entrepreneurial skills among small businesses and the broader community through counseling, training, research, advocacy and other resources and activities. —*Hawaii Business Research Library, Kihei, Hawaii*

These are just a few examples to give you some ideas. But there are countless other sources of ideas. Libraries are often entities within a larger entity, such as a college or university, corporation, or government agency or department. It is helpful to review the vision statement of your larger institution as well. Again, your aim is to use your web site to make these vision statements a reality.

Look again at the example from the Brooklyn Public Library. "Brooklyn Public Library will be a *vital center of knowledge for all*, accessible *24 hours a day*, and will be a leader in *traditional* and *innovative* library services which reflect the *diverse* and *dynamic* spirit of the people of Brooklyn." The emphasized words and phrases can be used when planning a web site: important information covering all areas of knowledge; the user base is everyone; 24/7; traditional *and* innovative services will exist side by side and both will be valued, as will diversity and dynamism.

How do you develop a mission?

Mission statements are more specific than vision statements. Here are some examples:

> An integral part of the educational program of the college, the library provides information resources and services to the college community. The primary purpose of the Wytheville Community College Library is to provide support for the educational goals of the college, as set down in the Catalog and Student Handbook of the college, by acquiring and maintaining a well-balanced, up-to-date collection of print, non-print, and electronic resources. Also of significant importance is the provision of information resources to the citizens of the college's service region.
> —*Wyethville Community College, Wyethville, Virginia*

> The College of St. Catherine Libraries, Audio-Visual Services and Archives exist to support the vision and mission of the College of St. Catherine. The Library serves as the information hub for a diverse community of learners on and off site. Through its services, facilities, collections, and equipment it supports and enriches the curricula, programs, and activities of the College.
>
> • It provides the college community with access to global information resources.

- It offers support and guidance in research methods, in the effective use of information technologies, and in the evaluation of sources.
- It strives to provide a setting in which collaborative learning is fostered and enhanced.

—College of St. Catherine Libraries, St. Paul, Minnesota

The El Segundo Public Library's mission is to meet the informational, educational, and recreational needs of the community in a welcoming environment. It provides organized collections, expert research staff, supportive services and access to additional resources through current technology and participation in cooperative library systems. The library fulfills its commitment to the future by providing stimulating materials and programs that encourage youth to become lifelong learners.

—El Segundo Public Library, El Segundo, California

The Mission of the Dallas Public Library is to link resources and customers to enhance lives. The Library is committed to inform, entertain, enrich, and to foster the self-learning process by facilitating access to its collections, services, and facilities to all members of the community. All service efforts will focus on customer expectations and needs.

The Library will make available a broad spectrum of ideas reflecting diverse points of view and will provide collections that reflect the need and diversity of the community it serves.

The Library will honor its public trust by assuring maximum use of public resources. Furthermore, the Library will stimulate the awareness and use of libraries to promote individual enlightenment, community enrichment, and economic vitality throughout the city.

—Dallas Public Library, Dallas, Texas

The mission of the Arkansas State Library is to serve as the information resource center for state agencies, legislators and legislative staffs, to provide guidance and support for the development of local public libraries and library services, and to provide the resources, services, and leadership necessary to meet the educational, informational and cultural needs of the citizens of Arkansas. The agency administers state and federal funds appropriated for libraries and library development, including State Aid to Public Libraries funds and federal Library Services and Technology Act (LSTA) funds (formerly Library Services and Construction Act).

—Arkansas State Library, Little Rock, Arkansas

The purposes of the National Freight Transportation Library are to preserve freight transportation history and to provide a central source of current information, statistics, decisions, texts and other literature serving the needs of the transportation/logistics profession, academia, students, librarians, journalists, governments and the public sector.

—*National Freight Transportation Library, Huntington, New York*

What should you be looking for in a vision or mission statement?

As you can see from the preceding examples, libraries use all sorts of styles for mission and vision statements. While reviewing your own mission and vision statements, you should be scanning for named groups of people and services. (These tend to be nouns and verb phrases.)

For example, here's a list of patron groups drawn from the examples just given:

Resident	Customers
Glen Ellyn residents	All members of the community
Preschoolers	
Seniors	State agencies
People of Brooklyn	Legislators
Communities of users	Legislative staffs
Individuals statewide	Local public libraries
Small businesses	Citizens of Arkansas
Broader community	Transportation/logistics profession
College community	
Citizens of the college's service region	Academia
	Students
Community of learners on and off site	Librarians
	Journalists
Youth	Governments
Lifelong learners	Public sector

And here's a list of services and goals. These aren't always so easy to figure out, and your mission statement may not be specific enough to provide them:

Lifelong learning

Leisure experiences

Introduce to information technology

Accessible 24 hours a day

Traditional services

Innovative services

Integrating technological advancements with traditional services

Support the provision of instruction

Communicate and conserve knowledge

Apply new technologies to assist users

Improve and optimize the library's systems

Support, enhance and inspire education, scholarship and service

Free and open inquiry

Developing entrepreneurial skills

Provide support for the educational goals of the college

Acquiring and maintaining a well-balanced, up-to-date collection of print, non-print, and electronic resources

Provision of information resources

Supports and enriches the curricula, programs and activities of the college

Provides . . . access to global information resources

Support and guidance in research methods, in the effective use of information technologies, and in the evaluation of sources

Meet informational, educational, and recreational needs

Organized collections

Expert research staff

Supportive services

Access to additional resources through current technology and participation in cooperative library systems

Providing stimulating materials and programs

Link resources and customers

Inform, entertain, enrich

Foster the self-learning process

Facilitating access to its collections, services, and facilities

Make available a broad spectrum of ideas

Provide collections that reflect the need and diversity of the community

Serve as the information resource center

Provide guidance and support for the development of local public libraries

Provide the resources, services, and leadership necessary to meet . . . educational, informational, and cultural needs

Preserve freight transportation history

Provide a central source of current information, statistics, decisions, texts and other literature

Picking out the salient parts of your vision and mission statements can help you to your next step—setting goals for your web site.

How do you set goals?

So, one day you decide to build a barn. How big will it be? Where will you locate it? From which kind of materials does it need to be built? How will you answer these questions without knowing *why* you are building a barn? Do you need to have it tall enough for a sailboat? Will it need to be warm enough to house farm animals? So it is with a web site. You need to know what the goals are before you can build it.

There are many examples of web sites that are goal-less (or should we say clueless?): the e-commerce site without an online shopping tool, the clip-art sites with links to general search engines, and, yes, library sites that try to be all things to all people instead of focusing on their own communities.

As you move along in the redesign process, you will often find yourself at a decision point. How will you inform that decision? By asking if it fits within the goals of your site. The ability to fall back on your goals document takes a great deal of the pressure off of the decision maker. Is there an item or a task that doesn't fit your goals? Then there's no need to keep it. If an item or a task does clearly fit your goals, then you should do it well for the user groups stated in your goals.

Depending on the size and diversity of your user group and on your mission, your goals may be few in number and straightforward or many and complex. In either case, the goals document should answer these questions: "Why do we have this web site, what will it do, and for whom?" Remember, this is not a vision statement, so don't be lofty, be real. You are taking your mission and vision statements and narrowing them to focus on your web site. Spend a paragraph talking about who the site is for and what it should accomplish. Go ahead and mention the Internet, since that's the reality of where the web site lives. An example of a goals statement follows.

Use your goals statement to help you make decisions as you move along in this process. It will help you decide which patron groups from chapter 5 and which tasks from chapter 6 to include. It can also be used later as a metric in your evaluation, which we describe in chapter 10. If your web site meets these goals, you'll be one step closer toward being able to say your site was successful.

A Sample Goals Statement

The Harrington Public Library web site serves the members of the Harrington Public Library community (community members who live within the boundaries of the library district) whether online at the library or from another location. The web site will provide the members with information about the library and its events, its collections, and its services. The web site will also, whenever possible, use the convenience of the Internet on behalf of its members by providing online access to library services. The library web site will take advantage of the global nature of the Internet on behalf of its user community by providing links to other high-quality Internet resources and information about the community it serves.

Finding the patron's conceptual model

Now that we're clear on what we want our site to do, we're going to turn around and look at the site from the user's point of view. One way to do that is to use a conceptual model.

The *conceptual model* is a kind of metaphor that you can use to make your site navigable and easy to use for your patron. It's a reference that the patron can use to make sense of your site. For example, consider the use of a shopping cart in an online store. The site designer was betting that you as a consumer knows what a shopping cart is and what to do with it. If the designer was a good designer, everything you do with that shopping cart is easy and intuitive, based on your previous experience with shopping carts. Online shopping sites use the retail store as their underlying conceptual model because they know consumers will understand it.

A library is its own conceptual model in our culture. Most people in the United States know what to expect of a library: shelves, books, magazines, newspapers, a catalog, a circulation or checkout desk, a reference or information desk, a librarian, a shelver, and so forth. Just be careful as a librarian and designer that you don't use *your* conceptual model of a library as a staff member. You have to use the patron's model! The differences are subtle, but they are there. Call things what the patrons call them (for example, most patrons don't know what "technical services" are).

The library conceptual model works for library sites because it translates well from bricks and mortar to the electronic environment. We use the library conceptual model throughout this book. If you switch metaphors and try to make your library a retail store, your patrons will only be confused and unhappy.

As anyone who has worked in a library will note, however, there are people who do not have a conceptual model of the library—young people who have become Google dependent or people who support the library but don't actually use it. Then there are people who, for whatever reason, have just never been into a library. Your library web site can help them understand the conceptual model if it follows the standard, cultural library model. Think of patrons in your bricks-and-mortar library. Some of them want to immediately ask for help, while others want to do it themselves. Library signage and layout tend to help both kinds of patrons. Over many years, standard terminology has helped lots of new library patrons, and the same will be true for your online patrons.

What's next?

Now that you've created a goals statement, you're ready to tackle the users for whom user-centered design is named. Chapter 5 is about patrons—who they are, how to classify them, and how to analyze the information you get about them.

Chapter 4 checklist

- Have you scanned your vision statement to identify patron groups?
- Have you scanned your mission statement to identify patron groups?
- Have you scanned your vision statement for possible goals and services?
- Have you scanned your mission statement for possible goals and services?
- Have you written a goals statement that you can use to measure future decisions against?
- Are you committed to using the patron's conceptual model?

NOTE

1. *Economist Business Encyclopedia Dictionary* at http://www.economist.com/encyclopedia/Dictionary.cfm?id=ID8A47DBBB-2F3F-11D5-8496-00508B2CCA66

PATRONS
Who They Are

5

This chapter is all about library patrons and how to find and analyze the information you'll need about them for your redesign (see fig. 5-1).

At the end of this chapter, you will understand:

- how to determine who your patrons are
- how to define "patron groups"
- what you need to know about your patron groups—and why
- which patron groups you should focus on cultivating
- when to focus on each patron group within the redesign cycle

Why is it important to know who our patrons are?

To prepare for redesign, we will need to target certain groups of patrons. Then we will need to decide redesign objectives for each group so we meet their specific needs.

PHASES and TASKS			
Set Site Goals	**Analyze Site**	**Redesign Site**	**Evaluate Site**
Review Mission and Vision	**Define Patrons, Tasks, and Library Objects**	Design Using Patrons and Tasks	Evaluate Site with Patrons

FIGURE 5-1
Redesign Process Chart—Patrons

In the previous chapter, we discussed the conceptual model and its importance to redesign. We also noted how the library conceptual model makes sense to librarians and library staff but may not be completely clear to patrons. Realizing that how we view the library and ways to find information comes from our library conceptual model, we now must specifically define our patrons and use their own conceptual models in designing our web site. To help our patrons achieve their goals, we need to be certain that our librarian conceptual model successfully intersects with the patrons' models within the library web site. Remember, the library site itself may often perform the intermediary role between the patron and the information. So we must redesign to assure that as much as we could do for patrons if we were personally interacting with them is placed within the site for their assistance.

If we design for the wrong patron groups, we will make a site for someone whose success does not affect our library's continued success.

Specifically determining our patrons allows us to define and keep focused on specific redesign objectives for those patrons. We will use each group's own conceptual model and behavior as the basis for redesign decisions.

Who are your patrons?

The following exercises will help you decide on which user groups you'll focus your redesign. It's a lengthy and often contentious process, but it's key to your redesign process, so take your time and be thorough. If consensus is not reached at this step, you should carefully note any dissension among team members—this probably either will be solved during the redesign process or will become an area to which you'll have to return.

The steps are: (1) broadly define all possible patron groups; (2) write patron profiles, or personas; (3) decide which keywords characterize each patron group; and (4) use these keywords to determine the accuracy of the patron group definitions.

Step 1: Defining patrons

Let's start by broadly defining all possible patron groups. What is a patron, exactly? Our definition of a patron for this analysis is someone who has a specific goal and personal characteristics that can be categorized in some way. Patrons are characterized by personal attributes and by their own behaviors, not by the tasks that they perform.

Because you represent a library, your patrons can be anyone. The term *anyone*, however, means *everybody*, and this is too broad a target for success.

We need to very carefully and narrowly define who visits as well as who uses the site. (In the next chapter we will define *how* they use the site.) Then we need to make decisions about which patrons are important to the library's success.

Note that not all visitors to your web site are going to actually use the library. Many visitors will have a patron role. Others may be browsing or looking at the site for other reasons. These visitors also may be important to your site.

We will be making composite patrons from our categorizing exercise. But at this point, don't worry about ranking patron groups by importance. We'll get to that.

WHERE TO GO FOR INFORMATION

You may have had discussions about patron groups already and know who comprises these groups. If not, you can find information about patron groups from your mission and vision statements, demographics, and patron records. To get started, keep a notebook of observations and query coworkers. Let people know you are going to do this, and ask them to think about it. A discussion is best because you want coworkers to support your redesign.

To define the users of a web site, a usability expert typically asks key players their opinion. Key players include management as well as those who interact with patrons. This includes reference librarians, circulation desk staff, library board members or library advisers, and any library staff person who works with the public and would like to offer an opinion.

Determining patron groups is a very political issue and could send your committee into a long discussion. The starting point is anyone named in your mission statement or goals.

In chapter 4, we described how the mission statement relates to the redesign process. The following mission statement example helps us discover who the patron groups are for an academic library.

Notice that faculty, students, and staff are all listed in the mission statement below and must therefore all be patron groups. Remember that sometimes potential user groups will not be defined in the mission statement.

Mission of the University Library

To support, enhance, and collaborate in the instructional, research, and service activities of the faculty, students, and staff, and contribute to the common good by collecting, organizing, preserving, communicating, and sharing the record of human knowledge.

—*University of Michigan Mission Statement*

Unnamed patron groups may be of importance to your library. Are you concerned about nonusers of the library? Do you have a board or donors who are important to your administrative structure or financial health? You may have an especially supportive group of faculty members who have high expectations, needs, or both. Perhaps you have users with disabilities. Another major area of concern is underserved populations who have social, economic, and educational needs different from those of the general population.

Take some time to look at your mission statement. Use your mission statement to compare the types of library visitors with the goals you are trying to accomplish. The process generally is not quick; it takes a lot of thinking and discussing as preparation for redesign. However, the more clearly you define your patrons in this step, the bigger will be your return for the site. We will also learn how to determine who is important in this chapter.

BROADLY DEFINE ALL POTENTIAL PATRON GROUPS

To do this, brainstorm a list of all possible groups, and use patron groups identified from the vision and mission statements. Don't be overly concerned about being accurate at this stage.

Public library patron groups might include the following:

Children, preteens (kindergarten–grade 6)

Home-schooled children

Young adults (grades 7–12)

Frequent library users

Donors to the library

Library volunteers

College students

Lifelong learners

Staff

Net surfers

Community characters

The underserved—migrants, the urban poor, ethnic groups, nonnatives or people who speak English as a second language, the homeless

Foreign students using the Internet to stay in touch with home

Meeting room users from the community

Board members

Here's an example of academic library patron groups:

Faculty

Graduate, doctoral students (academic researchers)

Staff

Undergraduate students—first two years

Undergraduate students—last two years

Adult undergraduates

University and college administrators (who are also funders)

Applied researchers

Adjunct faculty

Teachers

Visiting scholars

Human resource information seekers

Members of governing boards

Adult community members

Special-interest groups

Students (K–12) who live in the community

 The special collections library, which has a very large set of potential patrons, could include the following:

Special collection patrons

Funders

Board members

Academics

Applied researchers

Aficionados or fans who "just like the subject"

Visiting scholars

Management

EXAMPLE

Special Collections Library Patron Groups

To determine patron groups for the Turfgrass Information Center (TIC) online library, we brainstormed and came up with an initial list: it comprises all possible groups of patrons who we decided would visit the TIC web site:

Academic researcher in turfgrass-related subjects

Student in turfgrass-related subjects

CEO (turfgrass-related company or just interested in turf-
related activities)

United States Golf Association members

Turfgrass professional who could be a funder

Golf course superintendent

Consumer of turfgrass-related products

Counter person at Fred's Super Garden Emporium

Golf course architect

Critic who is anti-turfgrass

We discussed an additional group, board members, but decided they were basically funders because of their understanding of fund-raising issues as well as their continuing support for certain types of web site improvements that would contribute to our ability to attract funders. They were a type of "funder approval indicator"—if they could understand our redesign, we were fairly certain that potential funders would also understand.

The list was compiled after intense discussion about the similarities or differences among the patron groups. Some of the criteria used were: business, personal, or academic interest in the subject; extent of knowledge about the field (puns abound in turfgrass); purpose or goal in seeking information at the site; extent of involvement in funding or desire for improved library services; and even people who might stumble onto the site while Google-searching for general information about turfgrass.

Using the brainstormed list of possible patron groups in chapter 4, we now narrow by characteristics. Looking just at the possible patron groups for public libraries, for example, after removing the redundancies, we can create a new list of representative patron groups:

Adult patrons	Adult learners
Nonpatrons	Kids
Community members	Teens

We may decide, for example, that community residents, a previous category, really consists of those who use the library's community services and those who don't.

Note: If you have the resources to do so, be sure to include *all* patron groups. Don't leave any groups out. An unnoticed or small group of patrons might be or become really important to your site success, if not now, perhaps in the future. You may as well have the work done in case criteria change during the redesign process.

Step 2: Creating patron profiles

Patron or user *profiles* (also called *personas*) are a way of describing your patron groups while still keeping the individual patron real. They are of great value, especially when the site programmers do not have any direct contact with patrons. The programmers will refer to the profiles whenever they need to make a redesign decision and do not have access to a patron, a librarian, a subject matter expert, or any other team member who could answer a question about patrons' actual attitudes or behavior. Profiles act as placeholders for patrons within the redesign process when real individuals are not involved.

Create a composite representative for each of your patron groups to clarify your thinking about patron groups. Give this patron a name, an approximate age, and a profession or field of study or interest. Add some details about her or his hobbies. Then describe how she or he uses the library, including attitudes about learning, methods of finding information, and any other factors based on your own observations.

You can observe patrons while working at the reference desk or while helping users. You can also use focus groups and a suggestion box. Keep a notebook at the reference desk to jot down patron observations that may be useful for your profiles. Another method is to ask staff members who work with the public to jot down their relevant observations. There may be groups you don't observe but about whom you'd like to get more information. These groups will need to be surveyed, perhaps by phone or mail or through focus groups. A number of books are available that can help you design surveys and lead focus groups.

Now you are ready to create your profile. Be sure to make this profile an average person, about middle range in behavior for the group. For example, undergraduate students have a broad range of study or research habits. You would want to profile the most common type of undergraduate student you have observed. You're going to use the patron you create throughout the process we describe in this book, from design through evaluation. The following section provides examples of profiles.

SAMPLE PATRON PROFILES

As you read the following patron profiles, note their characteristics (think "adjectives"). Note that Sandra is a single-minded academic, Thad hasn't had much experience with the library's services, and Emily is shy and doesn't like to ask for help. In a public library setting, Miles represents most of your adult patrons, while Millie's needs mirror those of adult learners in your community. Marie uses the library to perform in a community role. Taylor represents all of the school-age children in your community (would that they were all so library friendly!). Esther is not a library patron but belongs in a defined group, nonetheless, to represent those people who do *not* use the library but from whom the library would like to have support and patronage.

Although your representative patron won't have every trait that your patron group has, that's fine. In the next chapter, your patron groups will acquire more characteristics as you work through analysis and design.

EXAMPLES

Academic Researcher

Sandra is a graduate student in music history. She will complete her master's degree in the spring and go straight into her Ph.D. program in the fall. Between programs she will spend some time in Salzburg, Austria, researching possible topics for her dissertation. Sandra is a regular library patron and is comfortable performing online searches and asking library staff for help. Sandra is an active member of the student sailing club and is musical director for the school's Gilbert and Sullivan society.

Undergraduate Student

Thad is an undergraduate student in his sophomore year. He hasn't decided on a major yet but is trying to decide between sports management and education. His freshman experience in the library was limited to meeting his friends there, attending a one-hour lecture on using the online catalog, and recording textbooks on tape in the Center for Students with Disabilities, which is housed in the library. Thad is very computer savvy and uses the Internet for all his research needs. Thad lives in a fraternity and is on the golf team.

Advanced Student

Emily is a senior in engineering. She has one favorite science-oriented online service with which she is very familiar. Her use of the library building is limited to using the reserves section and studying. Emily lives at home in a nearby town and commutes to campus each day. Emily is a voracious reader and an excellent student.

Adult Library Patron

Miles is a marketing manager in his late forties. He uses the library to find reviews and reports of consumer goods, software, and computer hardware and to use the Internet. His family uses the library sporadically to check out DVDs and do school projects. Miles is interested in home computing and is an antique car enthusiast.

Community Member Who Is a Patron

Marie is an avid gardener and reader who also volunteers as the events coordinator for the local garden club. She also reviews new gardening books.

Adult Learner

Millie has been retired from her publishing job for two years and has gone back to school to take some courses in archeology. The college library is inconvenient for her, so she uses the public library to support her research papers. Millie lives alone and has two cats. Her children are grown and live in the same town.

Child

Taylor is a middle school student who uses the library when he writes school papers and when his parents are there. He likes to use the library's Internet terminals and CD-ROM stations. Taylor won the library's bookmark contest and sometimes helps with the summer reading program. Taylor's family uses the library once a week or more to check out books.

Community Member Who Is a Nonpatron

Esther is a longtime community resident who rarely uses the library. She is a senior citizen who lives on a fixed income and considers the library's expansion plans unnecessary.

Researcher

Mark is a faculty member who is focused on TIC's specialized collection on turf-grass. He is always highly motivated to use this library. As a frequent patron, he is also an advanced or power searcher in his subject area. He often looks for citations about himself and realizes that this is considered "ego surfing," but he knows the value of monitoring his academic visibility. He is always interested in the extent of content available in any library he visits.

Student

Mike is a beginning student in golf course/turfgrass management. He wants reliable bibliographic data as well as content for some of the academic work he is expected to do. He's really looking, though, for factual information rather than deeper subject knowledge. Because his experience has been Internet based, he expects a web-style interface. As an infrequent patron, he does not want too many steps to find information he seeks.

Funder

Fred Funder is the CEO of a *Fortune* 500 company and a big fan of turfgrass—he might work in the turfgrass industry or perhaps is a golf fan who is interested in turfgrass. He is not particularly web-comfortable and probably will ask his assistant to find the information he needs rather than risk looking less than brilliant. He needs to be sure that if he has to use the site, he will always be successful. He is considering sending money to the endowment fund as a corporate sponsor.

WHAT IF PATRONS HAVE MULTIPLE ROLES?

They probably will, especially in public or academic libraries. For example, an older adult returning to school may be writing an academic paper on Shakespeare while also researching information on a new car and furthering his career by reading about new developments in robotics. Such a person has three different roles: first, as an academic researcher; then as a casual browser; and, finally, as an adult learner. Remember that goals can define patrons; because the person has three separate goals, three different types of patrons are represented.

Although multiple roles can initially make redesign scary, this complexity is accommodated by our design, which emphasizes the patron's need for freedom *and* control. Keep this point in mind as we go through the next three chapters. The trick here is to just assign multiple roles as they come up; treat the person as a separate entity every time he or she has a goal that doesn't fit within the original patron profile.

Step 3: Find the keywords that characterize each patron group

The patron profile describes physical, psychological, and behavioral characteristics as well as the environment in which the patron accesses your library. There will be categories of keywords that describe or characterize each patron group. Look through the patron profiles that you have written. Assign patron characteristics to all the groups. Then determine salient characteristics, or *keywords,* that either define or comprise an issue for each patron. Characteristics vary enormously with the web site, so we can't give you solid rules. You need to decide which characteristics are important for your own design. However, sample characteristics include the following:

> Cultural: background; first or acquired language
>
> Physical: age (mobility, coordination); accessibility issues (audio or text based, keyboard versus mouse, etc.)
>
> User experience: language level (first language, foreign language); Internet experience; knowledge of library procedures, including searching methods and expertise; frequency of library use
>
> Educational or reading level
>
> Behavioral or personality traits: comfortable with searching; shy
>
> Type of information sought (knowledge versus information)
>
> Access to equipment: screen resolution; Internet connection and download time
>
> Technology experience: comfort level with technology (using a mouse, for example); Internet experience

Many other characteristics are considered in usability, including environmental factors, such as ambient light, noise levels, or ergonomics, but this is beyond the scope of this book.[1]

Remember Miles, the forty-year-old marketing manager and public library patron we profiled earlier in the chapter? He would probably have the following characteristics:

> Physical: relatively fit and able to use keyboard and mouse
>
> Technology: high comfort level with technology
>
> Access to equipment: up-to-date computer equipment with relatively fast Internet connection and download time
>
> User experience: native English speaker; high Internet experience; some experience with library procedures, including searching; more comfortable with Google-type searching; somewhat frequent library usage

Type of information sought: information plus entertainment plus knowledge (*information* comprises facts and figures or a quick answer; *knowledge* is in-depth information, such as what you'd need to write a paper or to gain subject expertise)

For the Turfgrass special collections library, we handled this exercise a bit differently First, we wrote very short profiles for each of the site users with whom we were familiar. These profiles were based on observations by the library staff and were the outcome of a group discussion and agreement.

Then we combed through the profiles and decided to list the characteristics of the patrons, reviewed them along with any other salient characteristics we could think of, and tried to assign them to our entire list of proposed patron groups. The purpose, of course, was to see if we had some groups that were really the same group with different names.

Researcher: Highly motivated to use this library. Frequent user, probably an advanced searcher in subject area. Looking for his or her own work (ego surfing). Interested in the extent of the content available (scope). Needs power and control. Has "fire hose fear" (too much information at once).

Student: Wants reliable bibliographic data as well as content for academic work. Also looking for factual information rather than deeper subject knowledge. May expect a web-style interface. As an infrequent user, will not want too many steps to find information sought.

Funder: Not particularly web-comfortable; needs success on this site. In-depth subject knowledge may be an issue.

After working through these profiles, we compiled an initial set of characteristics for our special collections library patron groups:

Web savvy

Computer comfort level

Subject knowledge (Turfgrass)

Information versus knowledge

Connection speed

Frequency of use

Ego involvement (e.g., author search for self)

Content (extent available)

Need for power and control

Motivation level high

Fire hose fear (too much information at once)

Data reliability (bibliographic)

Data reliability (is content abstract/full text?)

Interface attractiveness

Step 4: Narrowing the focus

At first glance, your patrons may seem like a diverse bunch, but as you examine your data you'll determine that many different groups will have overlapping characteristics. There are probably fewer groups than you originally imagined. The last step in defining is to narrow the patron groups.

Reorganize the patron groups by similar characteristics; look for significantly common overlaps between groups to narrow down the actual number of patron groups.

Let's look closely to see whether your patron groups can be narrowed because they share similar characteristics. We are going to compare groups by characteristics to determine how many groups we really have.

First, make a list of your possible patron groups. For example, possible patron groups using an academic library might be the following:

Undergraduate students

Graduate students

Ph.D. candidates

Academics (faculty)

Returning older students

Special-interest groups (genealogists, retired faculty)

Students K–12

Next, enter these terms along the top of the patron groups chart shown in figure 5-2. Look at the characteristics of each group and then redetermine your groups. Reorganize the patron groups by similar characteristics; look for significantly common overlaps between groups to narrow down the actual number of patron groups.

Notice if you can either split up or more broadly define each patron group. For example, it seems as though the special interest group and the returning

	Proposed Patron Groups		
Academics (faculty)	Special-Interest Users	Returning Students Older Students	Undergraduate Students Students K–12

FIGURE 5-2
Academic Library Patron Group Chart Version 1

older students group are identical. We can collapse both groups into one group, now labeled special-interest/older students (see fig. 5-3).

Proposed Patron Groups → _Characterized by:_	Academics (faculty)	Special-Interest and Older Students	Undergraduate Students
Internet experience	Medium–High	Low–High	Medium–High
Knowledge of library procedures, including searching methods, expertise, or both	Low–High	Low–High	Low–High
Type of information sought (knowledge versus information)	Knowledge	Information and Knowledge	Information and Knowledge
Frequency—of library use	Frequent	Infrequent–Frequent	Infrequent–Frequent
"Comfort level" with technology (using a mouse, for example)	Medium–High	Low–High	Medium–High

Proposed Patron Groups—Academic Library

FIGURE 5-3
Academic Library Patron Group Chart Version 2

Note that while both academics and undergraduate students share many characteristics, one crucial difference is in the type of materials sought—knowledge versus information. We would not collapse these two groups. Common sense and experience in the library also tell us that we would not collapse any other groups further, although as we continue in redesign, we may split patron groups in other, more appropriate ways.

How do you select the patron groups you wish to target?

The first thing you may be asking yourself is, "How will I know who is important?" Politics and demographics can change the importance of your patron groups over time. If you are in a public library looking for more local funding, you may choose to move your nonpatron group or your families up in importance. An academic library at an institution that is changing from a four-year college to a university will need to move researchers into a new level of importance. So, too, a growth or decline in numbers within a patron group may indicate a need for change.

Now we have just a few well-defined groups. We need to narrow down again, this time to those we really wish to target. _Note:_ One of the advantages of reorganizing groups by characteristics is that some groups will be included within target populations. This means you will be helping additional groups of patrons. For example, if the original group of patrons called returning older students was not a targeted patron group, because it is now included within the new group, special-interest/older students, it will benefit from redesign also. In the future it may become a targeted group, and the initial analysis is ready and awaiting review or validation.

How do you choose just a few patron groups for your redesign focus?

Remember the discussion about politics and demographics? Patron groups may become more important or less important . . . if their roles shift. For example, in an academic library, undergraduates are most likely the biggest group in number, but alumni, researchers, or board members may be more influential. Don't forget important minorities.

Here are some examples of factors that may require narrowing of patron groups, based on preceding lists:

> Your community will add more computers to the library.

> The community college is teaching more classes about using the Web, so you know Google is going to get more popular, and you'll get more traffic from community college students.

> You live in a retiree community; the library's funding vote is important.

EXAMPLE

Narrowing

Here's an example of how we worked through the information to decide who the major patron groups for the special collections library would be.

First, we knew from our vision discussion (not included here) that one objective was delivery of quality information. We wanted those within the academic researchers group to understand that the library's reputation for reliable content was going to continue even though we were attracting other types of patrons to the site who were not academic researchers and who, in fact, were more interested in information.

We also wanted to keep the goal of encouraging the turfgrass students group to use this site and learn to consider it a crucial resource throughout their professional careers.

We knew potential funders from various groups would be coming to the site, and many of them would not be academic researchers. We decided to create a special group called funders and to assign to this group the lowest level of web savvy and other common areas (a more detailed discussion, which we will not cover in this book) that might hinder satisfaction with the site and therefore hinder endowment!

We decided to assume that a funder might need more assistance and visual cues. We also knew that because of widespread Internet use, consumers might eventually become patrons of this library. While we wanted to consider how to help them at some time, we realized that this was not an immediate redesign priority. However, we also realized that some of the characteristics of targeted groups like funder would be similar to consumers' characteristics, which allowed us to start some of the design for the consumer group now along with the funder group.

We also knew the golf association folks did not constitute a current group of users, but within a year, after we introduced the first changes to the site and made this site more known with our endowment campaign, they could potentially be visiting the site more frequently. We decided to plan for that change and redesign to make the changes in the site successful for them to use—this is another crucial area for our vision and goals.

After much discussion, which we'll not go into here, the special collections library final patron groups were reorganized into the following initial targeted set:

> Academics, including future academics (students)
>
> Architects, interested primarily in golf course design
>
> Golf association folks, interested primarily in maintenance

We recognized that other very distinct groups remained, but we were not able to narrow the groups any farther. However, like most libraries, our resources are limited. We then made a decision that these groups, some of which were quite important to the site's well-being, would not be part of the primary focus of our redesign for the next few years. Whenever resources made it possible, however, we would include the redesign considerations we had determined for them.

How many groups should you end up with?

Generally, targeted patron groups will number from three to six. Later on, during redesign as well as periodically during maintenance, you can review this selected set to decide who to target and who to "untarget."

Congratulations! When you have done this step, you will be certain of who you must attract and retain for library web site success.

Now, set up a redesign schedule

Success means choosing the groups that are most important to you and redesigning for them. You now know who you need to target.

Now, set up a redesign schedule that includes only targeted groups. Rank the patron groups by deciding the relative importance of each group to your library site's success *over time*. Decide as far ahead as you can exactly when redesign for each group is needed. You will use this schedule throughout your web site's life and whenever you need to make substantial changes to the site; if this preplanning is in place when you are redesigning, you can anticipate it and accomplish it more easily when the time comes.

EXAMPLE

Redesign Schedule

Figure 5-4 shows a sample redesign schedule (project timeline) for the TIC. It shows the broad, phased plan for redesigning by patron group.

Redesign Schedule—Patron Groups Inclusion			
Add Group Golf Association Members ────────▶			
Add Group Golf Course Architects ────────▶			
Current Patron Group Academic Researchers ────────▶			
Year: 2000	2001	2002	2003

FIGURE 5-4
Turfgrass Redesign Schedule

Begin to think about these patron groups and about what each group's set of expectations for the site might be. We will discuss what the patrons actually do and what that will mean to our site redesign in the next two chapters.

What's next?

Chapter 6 introduces and discusses patron behavior. We'll finish the analysis phase in chapter 7 with the final piece, library objects. Chapter 8 focuses on whether to design from scratch or redesign and discusses specifically how to redesign by targeted group. And then it's on to chapter 9, where we put the interface together.

Chapter 5 checklist

- Do you have a list of all possible patron groups, both present and future?
- Have you assigned characteristics to all these patron groups?
- Have you narrowed or broadened your patron groups by characteristics?
- Have you determined the relative importance of each patron group to your site?
- Have you determined which are now and which will be your targeted patron groups?
- Have you made a site redesign timeline detailing when you will focus on each patron group?

NOTE

1. See Hackos and Redish.

TASKS
Understanding What Patrons Want to Do

6

This chapter discusses patron behavior, another key area we'll need for redesign. Steps that patrons follow to accomplish a goal comprise a *task;* you may have heard of or even used task analysis in your own work (see fig. 6-1).

At the end of this chapter, you will understand:

- why it's important to determine exactly what patron groups want to do
- how to determine what patron groups want to do
- how to decide which tasks are worth including
- how to determine the order in which patrons wish to do these tasks
- how to make it easy for patrons to do these tasks

PHASES and TASKS			
Set Site Goals	**Analyze Site**	**Redesign Site**	**Evaluate Site**
Review Mission and Vision	**Define Patrons, Tasks, and Library Objects**	Design Using Patrons and Tasks	Evaluate Site with Patrons

FIGURE 6-1
Redesign Process Chart—Tasks

Why is it important to know what patrons do?

As just noted, we call the steps that patrons will perform in the library in order to meet a goal "tasks." Examples of tasks could include searching for a book, sending an email, putting an item on reserve, booking a room for a community meeting, or requesting an interlibrary loan. Tasks are anything that patrons want to do or should be able to do at your library. The order in which they perform a task is called a *taskflow*. A series of tasks to achieve a more complicated goal is called a *workflow*, although these terms are often used interchangeably.

Knowing patron tasks and workflows is *crucial* to the success of your web site. There's an inherent problem in many site designs, and it occurs when flexibility is not built into the design. (Lack of flexibility means it's more difficult to change the design, but, more importantly, it means that patrons may not be able to navigate the site.) For site success, we want to incorporate flexibility in the design. That's done by focusing and designing the navigation for the site by indirectly incorporating the patrons' tasks rather than by relying on building paths through the interface by task. (Don't worry if this doesn't make sense yet; chapter 7, "Library Objects," will explain this thoroughly.)

Now, for each patron group you have identified, you need to determine the following about their tasks and workflows:

> Which patron groups perform what tasks
>
> How important these tasks are to each group
>
> How often groups perform these tasks

Let's go on to defining tasks; we'll discuss the three preceding criteria and their importance in detail later in this chapter.

How do we determine what patrons do?

How do you know exactly what patrons do? To learn how someone does something, the oldest and most efficient method is to observe the person doing the task. With a library site, there are several good reasons to do this.

First, you're not the person who does the task. For many reasons, the way you do the task as a librarian will not be how a nonlibrarian patron does the task. You might have performed the task many times, or you may have advanced training in how to do the task, so you have shortcuts built into your process. As a librarian, for example, you know many search techniques. Patrons who are not librarians or who are not otherwise specifically trained to search, however, may have another conceptual model, like Google. They will not know the difference between a journal and a magazine, or what *database* really means, or the difference between a Boolean OR and an AND. The difference between *keyword* and *subject* is completely meaningless to many library patrons.

Another reason you want to observe, and the reason designers like to gather observations about performing a task, is that sometimes you can improve the design by incorporating novel ways to perform the tasks. There is a great deal to be said for anecdotal evidence or the Eureka! moment. In software development this kind of observation and design information often provides both the genius and the impetus for new, advanced functionality. While this statement generally applies to complicated web sites, web applications, or the development of actual software applications for computers, it is true in any design situation.

Redesign Tip: Don't assume that you know how people do their tasks. There is nothing better than actual observation.

This may be obvious, but be sure to take the best notes you can. Nothing is more frustrating than trying to decipher some hurriedly scribbled notes that were clearly important to you at the time—just look at those exclamation marks!!—and now you haven't a clue about the great insight you had. If you are observing patrons with specific skills (say, advanced researchers), see if you can contact them for further discussion when you are working on your analysis and a question comes up.

Very occasionally, if the patron who represents the task you wish to map is really articulate, you may be able to ask how she or he does the task (the patron might mentally walk through the task and list the steps).

Gathering information about patrons and tasks is a lot of work. We've included some guidelines in this book to help you get started.

How do we determine tasks?

Where do you start? Well, based on our combined experience in web sites and applications, searching, and elibraries, here is our overview of what all web site users can do at the highest level:

> Enter
>
> Browse to see what's there *or*
>
> Search for a specific item or task
>
> Review the results of their search or browsing
>
> View one item of the results in detail, one at a time
>
> Do something with whatever they've found (fill it out, discard it, purchase it, save it, renew it, add it to a cart or list, bookmark it, print it, email it, annotate it)
>
> Exit

Next, we need to study tasks that are specific to our library.

EXERCISE

Listing Patron Tasks

Make a list of all the tasks (by task title) that you can think of that patrons do in your library. Start with each targeted patron group and list their tasks. Then go on to the next patron group and list all their tasks until you've worked your way through all the groups.

You might want to make a straight list of tasks or perhaps be more efficient and put together a table of tasks by patron (later on you'll need to do this step anyway), since many patron groups will be performing tasks that are similar or identical.

Don't worry if more than one patron group is performing the same type of task; one of the things we need to determine is how many patron groups are doing the same task.

Here's an example to help; it's a starter list for a public library showing some of the many tasks performed by patrons (our source was the user profiles in chapter 5):

 List of tasks by patrons

> Find reviews/reports
>
> Use Internet
>
> Check out videos or DVDs
>
> Do school projects
>
> Do research projects
>
> Get books
>
> Check out books
>
> Renew books
>
> Pay fines
>
> Read magazines
>
> Read newspapers
>
> Study
>
> Hang out with friends
>
> Participate in summer reading program
>
> Use community rooms

From the preceding list, we've made a Task by Patron chart like the one in figure 6-2.

Patron Groups and Their Tasks					
	Patron Group				
Task Title	*Adult*	*Adult Learner*	*Child*	*Comm. Nonpatron*	*Comm. Patron*
Find reviews/reports					
Use Internet					
Check out videos or DVDs					
Do school projects					
Do research projects					
Get books					
Check out books					
Renew books					
Pay fines					
Read magazines					
Read newspapers					
Study					
Hang out with friends					
Participate in summer reading program					
Use community rooms					

FIGURE 6-2
Tasks by Patron Groups Chart Version 1

All right, that wasn't so bad, was it? When you start to think this way, it's fairly quick to list the tasks that are going on in your library.

As we mentioned, there's some overlap between tasks here, and that's good. That overlap is important to us, and we're going to narrow by comparison of characteristics, just like we did in chapter 5, as we simplify, simplify, simplify.

What are scenarios?

Scenarios are a set of tasks, and we've already talked about them a little. All of the patron profiles we've written have talked about the activities patrons perform at libraries. Specific activities or sets of tasks with only one goal comprise scenarios. Probably the most common scenario for a library would be "get a book."

We'll be coming back in detail to scenarios. They form the basis for designing as well as evaluating.

How do we look at tasks in detail?

Now, we're going to go through these examples so that you can practice thinking about tasks in detail. Later in this chapter we'll discuss which tasks need detail.

The following list shows specific examples of patron tasks found in each of our example libraries (these tasks may apply to more than one type of library). We're going to give them task titles (for example, Ask a Reference Question) because we'll be selecting and looking at the most important tasks for our library patrons in detail as part of redesign, and we need to think of each of these tasks as specific little scenarios that we'll use again and again during the design process.

> *Public library:* Ask a Reference Question
>
> *Special collections library:* Request an Interlibrary Loan
>
> *Academic library:* Place an Item on Reserve

EXAMPLE

Sample Task:
Ask a Reference Question

Millie is going to ask a question. If she were in the library itself, she'd approach a librarian, perhaps at a reference desk, and ask the librarian her question. Since Millie is at the electronic library, she's using email and a web form.

Millie is first looking for a place on the library web site where she can ask a reference question, which is exactly what she'd be doing at the physical library. Because the electronic library is a little different from real life, she knows that she can look for an FAQ (frequently asked question), found in a list of posted commonly asked questions, to see if there is general information about how to get her answer.

In the physical library, Millie would ask a librarian the question. Online, she finds a reference email form to fill out and send. This is akin to using a "virtual reference desk."

Millie wonders as she fills out the form if the virtual reference desk is staffed and whether her questions will just go into cyberspace, never to return answered. In real life, she could either deduce from the librarian's attitude, from a sign posted on the desk, or through a real conversation with the librarian how soon she would get an answer. In cyberspace, Millie checks around the virtual reference desk, but there isn't any specific information about how often questions are reviewed and answered, so she writes her reference question in the blank form.

Millie includes when she needs the answer and how best to reach her.

Millie sends her question. At this point, she expects either an answer or a clarification from the librarian (in which case she will loop back until she gets an answer).

Millie's goal could be written as follows: *Goal:* get answer to reference question (note that the actual goal is not to ask a question but to get the correct or appropriate answer).

Here are Millie's steps in general:

1. Look for place where she can ask a question
2. Look for a shortcut (FAQ) to save time about how to ask a question
3. Find a form to fill out to email a question
4. Fill out form, asking a question and supplying contact information, when due, and so on
5. Send email asking a question

In chapter 9, we will use this set of tasks directly in redesigning our web site.

How do tasks form a workflow?

We can make this into a workflow so that we'll have the steps in front of us for our design:

1. Patron Millie looks for a place where she can ask a question.
2. She might look for a shortcut (FAQ) to save time about how to ask a question.
3. She finds a form to fill out to email a question.
4. She fills out the form, asking a question and supplying contact information, when the answer is due, and so on.
5. She sends an email asking a question.

Just listing the numbered steps in the task is sufficient. For complicated tasks or sets of subtasks, usability experts often make workflow charts, which look like a flow diagram and which help them keep track of all the steps, backtracking, and so forth (see fig. 6-3).

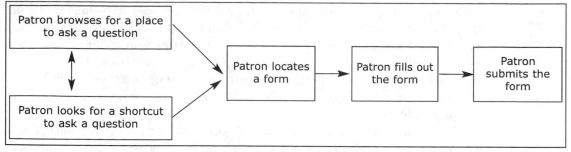

FIGURE 6-3
Workflow

Here's another example for the public library:

EXAMPLE

Sample Task:
Reserve a Community Meeting Room

Marie would like to use a community meeting room for her New Garden Books group. That is the goal of her recent trip to the library.

Marie goes to the library, looks over information about available rooms and dates, looks over the new garden books, suggests a few books the library should purchase, signs up for a room, and posts a notice on the bulletin board for the meeting.

Let's list every activity related to booking a room for the garden club in the preceding scenario, starting after Marie enters the library:

1. Look for available room
2. Look for available date
3. Sign up for room and date

What details can we surmise about Marie's task, since we are familiar with what must be done? Let's add these subtasks to the list now:

4. Supply contact information for room and date
5. Receive confirmation about room and date

Finally, let's go back to our scenario to list more tasks:

6. Post a notice about the meeting
7. Look for new books about gardening
8. Suggest two new gardening books

An important thing to remember is that each task should have only one goal. Now, notice two facts from the preceding example. First, Marie's goal is to set up a book club meeting at the library. In reading the paragraph about her activities while at the library, we see that several other activities not directly related to that goal are included. We should take them out of our list because we're refining the list to include only those steps that are specific to the Reserve a Community Meeting Room scenario.

The second fact is that we have added some subtasks, or broken the task out into a more detailed set of steps. This is exactly what we will need for both designing and testing and is something that we'll do for every task considered really important by the targeted patrons of our library (we won't bother for those tasks that we've decided are not important).

By preparing detailed examples of important tasks for targeted patrons, when we design we will have a scenario that enables us to replicate what steps are needed for a patron to successfully and easily reserve a community meeting room. If we have any trouble replicating those exact steps, then we can revise our design at that moment and save much effort later when we've less time and resources.

Also, should we decide to perform usability testing, we can use Reserve a Community Meeting Room as a test or evaluation scenario. (We'd tell a test participant, "Using this site, reserve a meeting room for your community event" and learn about how well we did by observing the participant's actions as she or he attempts to achieve this goal.)

How do we incorporate tasks in our web design?

How do we determine which tasks are worth including? You may not be able to or want to include all the tasks that patrons want to do. So how do you decide which ones you'll focus on when designing? The goals statement you created in chapter 4 will help you decide. Ask yourself, "Does this task fit within the goals of the web site?" If the answer is yes, add it to your redesign document. If the answer is no, move on and don't lose any sleep. You may wish to stash such tasks away for another look sometime in the future.

In what order do patrons need to do these tasks?

Well, looking at our earlier sample list, with the obvious exception of "enter" and "exit," visitors could be doing nearly any of the tasks in any order.

Here's a critical point to remember about this process: even though there is a lot of discussion in this book about "roles" or "tasks," we aren't proposing a redesign based primarily on roles. In real life, you might enter the library and perform several roles that have separate types of tasks—for example, you might be checking out a video, doing some serious research, or just looking at a community events calendar. We don't want you to get locked into the kind of navigation that often exists on web sites, where you literally have to go back to the home page and sequentially start over every time your role changes and you need to do disparate tasks. Because we don't define a site by roles and make roles the primary means of navigation, you won't have to worry very much about the order in which things are done.

Note that teens and kids are not really roles; usually libraries categorize these patrons by content that is published for them. (A teen or really bright kid could have the same characteristics as an adult patron, after all.)

Are you completely bewildered right now? Maybe an analogy would help. Think of it this way: a library is kind of like a grocery store.

Think about how the grocery store (any grocery store that's fairly large, say, ten aisles) is laid out. There are big aisles in parallel, with signs hanging over the aisles. You might be back in the corner purchasing frozen food when you remember that you need some cleaning products. What do you do? You look up for the sign that says Cleaning or Soaps or something similar, and you head over there. If the specific grocery store is familiar to you, you won't need much direction, and, in fact, you might have already written a list that takes the physical layout of the store into account. However, if the store is unfamiliar, you will most likely depend on visual cues, not only the items in the aisles but also the signs hanging above the aisles.

Now, although grocery stores have books and periodicals, they aren't libraries. And they certainly aren't web sites. But here's a question: Do you have to think very hard when you go to a grocery store to accomplish your goal of getting items? Generally not. Why is that?

In a grocery store, the shelves are often much higher than the customers, and you are almost in a maze when shopping, but you can "see" where everything is, all the time, by referring to the signs, so the time you spend being lost is minimized. You don't often feel really, completely lost in a grocery store, do you? No. Your frustration level stays pretty low, so you continue to seek items while sometimes browsing, too. At any point you can refer to the signs to determine where something can be found.

Another point about a grocery store: you do not always have a set path unless, of course, you are familiar with the store as just noted.

If you have time to browse the layout of an unfamiliar grocery store, you might methodically roam the aisles from one side of the store to the other, or circle the perimeter, or go to the back immediately, and so on, not paying attention to the signs because (1) you're not in a hurry, and (2) you want to explore, and with nothing specific to seek, there is no chance of losing your way. In other words, you do not have a set of tasks to do, such as "pick up ingredients for potato salad."

In fact, if you are familiar with the store, it's because you know where the items already are, and so they are "visible" in your conceptual model of the store.

Okay, compare a grocery store to a library. Customers want items. Patrons want items. Customers sometimes know exactly what they want and sometimes just want to browse and see what's available, perhaps for another time. Customers want to take items home and must go through a checkout system so that the grocery store knows what to restock. Sound like a library?

Now, keep the grocery store in mind. We'll come back to it.

How will we make it really easy for patrons to find what they want?

We make it easy by leaving the design open-ended, so patrons are free to choose what they do in whatever order they like, at any time. (*Note:* Remember the usability principles listed in chapter 2? This is number three.)

Now, let's put the discussion from chapter 3 about items into context, starting with the grocery store model. How do tasks happen in a grocery store? Customers are free to roam in any direction, change direction, double back, and look for an item by referring to a sign or by just going to that item. Until customers get to the checkout, an area where they must perform the sequential checkout task, they can do anything with grocery store items in any order they like.

We are going to provide a web site that basically models—looks and acts like—the real library. It won't force patrons to do things in any particular order. It will provide signs that patrons will use as guideposts or visual references for navigation. Take a few minutes to think about how that might be possible, based on what you've learned so far.

How do we reduce task information by patron group to the most important?

There's a lot of information you need to collect about patrons and tasks. Usability experts often use a table to initially look at the patrons and tasks and to determine which groups perform what tasks.

We started to answer this question by making a Task by Patron table earlier in this chapter. When the table is completed, you'll be able to quickly ascertain how common a task is to all patron groups. Tasks that have many patrons in common are probably important tasks. Let's assume that for now.

List the tasks by patron group. Then decide which tasks to target. Remember the other two criteria you can use to determine the significance of the tasks? They were: How important are these tasks to each group? and How often do patrons perform these tasks?

You will need to rank the tasks in each patron group and decide which ones are really important to them. For example, suppose a patron is visiting your library web site to ask questions that might more easily be answered by accessing a government site. You could note that and make a design decision that helps point that patron to more appropriate resources for official government information on the Web rather than replicate government web site information on your site. Look closely at frequency: a high number of patrons asking for certain information might initially appear to be a task that is important; however, it may be seasonally important (see the following paragraph) or just an artifact of web searching (our example is "Britney Spears" being the term most often searched by Google).

Information about school schedules as well as tax forms come to mind. Tax information might be important at certain times of the year, and you may choose to provide links to downloadable U.S. income tax forms on your library's home page from January 15 until April 15, for example; the rest of the year, tax information would be placed in a less prominent position. (And this very infrequent use of the library might be important to Esther, our nonpatron from chapter 5, whose approval, if not patronage, we need for our library's continued health.)

Some tasks are performed infrequently but are very important to a patron group. For example, in the special collections library, Fred Funder might visit the library site once a year (and his task comprises visit the library site, that's all). By task frequency standards, anything pertaining to Fred shouldn't qualify as important. But the special collections library's existence may depend on Fred's patronage in the form of funding, so having the information Fred would like to see on the library's home page taking up space for 364 unnoticed days of the year pales because on day 365 Fred visits the site, is thrilled to see what he expects to see, and donates generously. We'll call Fred's task, visit the library site, "infrequent but important." Of course, this brings up an important point: political or diplomatic tasks often need to be factored into web design.

EXAMPLE

Task List

Finally, we're going to go back, look at our public library task list, and show you what the Task by Patron table will tell us about our public library (see fig. 6-4). Much work has been done. We've now determined that these tasks are most important or most frequently used.

Task Title	Patron Group				
	Adult	Adult Learner	Child	Comm. Nonpatron	Comm. Patron
Find reviews/reports	X				X
Check out videos or DVDs	X	X	X		
Do school projects	X		X		
Do research projects		X			
Get books		X	X		X
Check out books		X	X		X
Participate in summer reading program			X		
Use community rooms					X

Patron Groups and Their Tasks

FIGURE 6-4
Task by Patron Groups Chart Version 2

What's next?

Chapter 7 will add one more consideration to our analysis; then we'll start redesigning.

Chapter 6 checklist

- Have you made a list and determined all tasks your targeted patrons will want to do at your web site?
- Have you listed these tasks by patron groups?
- Have you narrowed or broadened tasks by patron groups?
- Have you determined the relative importance of these tasks?
- Have you determined which tasks by patron groups you will focus on in redesigning?

LIBRARY OBJECTS

7

You'll be glad to know that we have only one more step in the analysis part of our redesign process chart, and also that it's the most fun and rewarding step (see fig. 7-1). In this chapter, you'll learn all about library objects, which are crucial to the redesign process and comprise the last piece we need for analysis. We're going to decide which library objects are needed within the web site.

So far, we have assembled from chapters 4 through 6 the following items: a mission or vision statement from our library; a list of goals for the site; a list of targeted patrons; goals these patrons have (what they come to the library to do); and tasks (specific steps that these patrons want to do in order to accomplish their goals). These five items comprise goals, patrons, and activities.

Now we need to decide exactly what patrons will *use* when they visit the library. This is even more important than what they will *do* because our redesign is constructed around a physical modeling of the library that is as close as we can make it to patrons' conceptual models. To make that model, we must find everything with which patrons interact.

PHASES and TASKS			
Set Site Goals	**Analyze Site**	**Redesign Site**	**Evaluate Site**
Review Mission and Vision	**Define Patrons, Tasks, and Library Objects**	Design Using Patrons and Tasks	Evaluate Site with Patrons

FIGURE 7-1
Redesign Process Chart—Library Objects

At the end of this chapter, you will understand:

- how to define a library object
- where to find library objects
- how to identify library objects for types of patrons
- how to work with object views
- what to do with library objects

What are library objects?

Each page in our web site will have certain types of elements that are familiar to patrons. These elements will be defined as *anything that patrons will manipulate and everything or everybody in the library with which patrons will interact.* We are going to draw a term, objects, from the software development world and call our elements *library objects*. (Using "objects" rather than "elements" will keep this part of the analysis more concrete and easier to envision.)

We're going to discover that there are many library objects in our patrons' conceptual model. Not all the library objects we find will be equally important to our patron groups. If this sounds familiar, then you're probably thinking (correctly) that we will identify them, narrow the list of library objects to those most important or frequent, and learn how to represent or characterize them. Farther along, we'll discuss their crucial importance in redesign.

Where do we find library objects?

Let's start looking for these library objects. We'll drag them all out and then decide which to feature within the electronic library.

Ask yourself this question, strange as it seems: What things do patrons "use" in the library? Here's a hint: library objects are usually nouns.

The first place to look is in the library itself. You can walk around the library and describe the library objects as you see them.

Let's pretend we're in the library, standing around and looking at everything that is there and thinking about the things we can do in the library.

You might want to start listing the library objects in your own library; this list can serve as a scratch sheet or reference for your own redesigning.

Another place that's often very revealing and will provide many library objects is the list of goals for the site. What library objects can be found in the list you've been compiling?

Finding Library Objects in a Goals Statement

Do you remember the purposes in Harrington Public Library's goals statement in chapter 4?

> provide information about the library
>
> provide information about the library's events
>
> provide information about the library's collections
>
> provide information about the library's services
>
> provide links to other high-quality Internet resources and information

There are library events, library collections, library services, information about the library, and links to Internet resources. Not a bad start.

These seem to be objects in the Harrington Public Library:

> Library information
>
> Library events
>
> Library collections
>
> Library services
>
> Access to Internet content
>
> Access to library services

Very good! Of course, to have "library resources" and "library services," you have to have "library," also. See how this works? To have "online access to services," you must have "services."

We might want to further explain what library resources are available. That will give us a list of more potential library objects.

Let's start making a big list of everything that might be a library object, based on what we've thought about so far:

Access	(Library) services
Use	Customers
Library resources	Self-service

Access   Library events

Web-based content   Library news

Web-based services   Library opportunities

The library itself

Amazing! Let's keep going.

Yet another place to look for library objects is within patrons' conceptual models, by taking a look at what those patrons expect to find in a library. We've chosen Mark, a special collections library patron and an advanced searcher (researcher) from chapter 5, to illustrate first, using his profile.

EXAMPLES

Library Objects Used by a Researcher

Recall Mark is a faculty member with a very specialized interest in turfgrass. He is always highly motivated to use this library. As a frequent patron, he is also an advanced or power searcher in his subject area. He often looks for citations about himself and realizes that this is considered "ego surfing," but he knows the value of visibility for getting tenure at the university. He is always interested in the extent of content available in any library he visits.

Now, aside from the first and most obvious library objects like "turfgrass," "content," "subject area," "patron," "advanced or power searcher," and "library," which we can add to our list, we also have located this: "citation" (about himself). Note that "tenure," although a noun, relates more accurately to Mark than to the library. Note also that the other most important library object is, of course, a "search," but the intricacies of designing a search are beyond the scope of this book.

Library Objects Used by a Funder

Here is another example with a novice patron, Fred Funder, who comes from our special collections library example in chapter 5 but who also may represent anyone whose financial or political patronage might benefit the library, whether academic, public, or special.

As you will recall, Fred Funder is the CEO of a *Fortune* 500 company and a big fan of turfgrass. He's not particularly web-comfortable and probably will ask his assistant to find the information he needs rather than risk looking less than brilliant. He needs to be sure that if he has to use the site, he will always be successful. He is considering sending money to the endowment fund as a corporate sponsor.

Fred's library world isn't very complicated. It comprises these library objects:

Fortune 500 company

Turfgrass

Money (endowment fund, corporate sponsor)

We see there's not much about acquiring knowledge, but Fred is a fan of our library's mission, and we want him to have a pleasant experience at our library. For Fred, our design implication will be to make this site as easy to use as possible.

Library Objects Used by an Adult Patron

Finding library objects in the public library isn't difficult. For our third example, let's add to our list of library objects those found in Miles's library world. Remember Miles? Miles is a marketing manager in his late forties. He uses the library to find reviews and reports of consumer goods, software, and computer hardware and to use the Internet. His family uses the library sporadically to check out DVDs and do school projects. Miles is interested in home computing and is an antique car enthusiast.

Semantics aside, we have the following list of library objects:

Reviews	Library
Reports	DVDs
Consumer goods	School projects
Software	Home computing
Computer hardware	Antique car enthusiast
Internet	

Miles has a more complicated library world than most patrons because he's got many additional uses for a library besides research, ego, or funding. Try some rearranging so that you build a conceptual model that approximates Miles's library world. Group them however you like.

Possible logical groups are:

Consumer goods (reviews, reports)

Computers (Internet, hardware, software, home computing)

Hobbies (DVDs, antique cars, reviews, reports)

School projects (library, reports)

Hmmm . . . wouldn't Miles's world have reviews and reports in school projects? Is Miles doing his daughter's homework, or would "school projects" belong to another patron (his daughter)?

Thinking a little more about this, Miles would probably look at periodicals (he'd call them magazines) for reviews and reports on consumer goods.

We might need a little more information about Miles's "computers" category: Does he use the Internet to find out about all those items, or does he also look at magazines to find out about them? Would he come to the library to use the computer and find out about both the "consumer goods" and the "computers" categories? Maybe he'd look through magazines or use the Internet while accompanying his young daughter, who is doing homework or attending story hour. We might ask him additional questions or find another patron similar to Miles and make a composite profile based on the most common goals that best fit our library's mission, rounding out our public library adult patron persona.

One other question about Miles: Is he going to school so that he needs research materials for reports?

Note: At this point, you're glad to have had that follow-up chat with Miles so you can refine your redesign.

Redesign Tip: You can do the next two steps in either order, depending on which way is easier for you. We've found that people often prefer one over the other. For us, it's easier to keep writing lists and then narrow each list until we get all the information out of our system and onto paper. And always *after* a break!

Our library object listing is growing. Here's some of our thought process:

> . . . um . . . consumer goods reviews, consumer goods reports, software reviews, software reports, hardware reviews, hardware reports, home computing, antique cars = stuff I can look up at the library or check out magazines for . . . let's call this category Articles/Magazines.

> . . . Internet—something I can use at the library; something I use at home to access the library . . .

> . . . DVDs . . . something I can select, check out, and take home . . .

> . . . Homework—something I do by using the Internet, Google, articles online; might be something I do by using a computer with word-processing capabilities at the library if I don't have a home computer . . .

Remember, this is brainstorming. Don't worry about this list right now and whether it's complete. There are a lot of library objects or maybe characteristics of library objects that we can use as the basis for our next step.

We brainstormed the initial list in figure 7-2 some time ago and present it here so you can see what a typical list looks like. Use this as a starter for your library object list if it helps. Note that we brainstormed across library categories, but your list should be a lot easier to make up. (And kindly let us know if we've missed any library objects.)

Brainstorming—Potential Library Objects	Type of Library				
A library might contain any of these things:	Special	Public	Academic	Kids	Teens
"Circulation"	X	X	X		
Articles	X	X	X	X	X
Bibliographies					X
Board of Directors	X	X	X		
Books	X	X	X	X	X
Books on Wheels (bookmobile)		X		X	X
Branch Catalogs		X	X		
Café, Internet Café					
Card Catalog	X	X	X	X	X
Community Calendar Information	X	X		X	X
Community Events Information		X		X	X
Databases					
DVDs (DVDs, movies)		X		X	X
Email	X	X	X	X	X
Endowment, Annual Foundation Appeal	X		X		
Help			X		
Information about the Community (college, city, etc.)		X			X
Interlibrary Loan	X	X	X		
Internet Availability	X	X	X	X	X
Journals	X	X	X		
Kid's Corner				X	
Library	X	X	X	X	X
Library Book Renewal	X	X	X	X	X
Library Branches		X	X		
Library Card = Login?	X	X	X	X	X
Library Events		X		X	
Magazines/Periodicals	X	X	X	X	X
Main Library		X	X	X	X
My Library Account	X	X	X	X	X
Newspapers		X	X		
Read to Me Schedule (story times for kids)		X			X
Reference	X	X	X		
Research			X		
Reserves			X		
Services for the Blind		X	X	X	X
Special Reading Lists (summer, best-sellers)		X		X	X
Study Guides			X		X
Subject Index	X				
Teenager Corner					X
Type of Branch		X			

FIGURE 7-2
Library Objects Brainstorming List

What comprises a library object?

All right, now you have a list of the possible library objects that your patrons use. (It's probably a big, unwieldy list.)

Some of the library objects in the list, however, aren't really library objects. They are pieces of a library object and will need to be grouped, or put back, with their original library object.

And some of the library objects could be more logically grouped into sets of library objects. This sounds awful perhaps, but librarians do this kind of classification work all the time, and our observation is they generally like it, so you might enjoy this part of the exercise.

When you finish these steps, you'll have a little, wieldy list. But how? Look through it and reorganize. Think of the following when you're examining lists like these: "This library object has a/n _____." For example, "This (Main) library has six branch libraries" or "This reserve area has books and periodicals." Looking over our list in figure 7-2, we note that Articles are part of Magazines/Periodicals and Journals. Bibliographies belong to Books.

Do we really have to narrow and broaden again?

Ugh! Does this get easier? It sure does or we wouldn't bother doing this process either. Here are more detailed examples for you—and you are very nearly done, as soon as this becomes clear. We now regroup the objects in the table in figure 7-2. Here's some of the process. A library might contain any of these things:

> Board of Directors; Endowment, Annual Foundation Appeal; Information about the Community (college, city, etc.)

> Books; "Circulation"; Bibliographies; Card Catalog; Databases; DVDs (DVDs, movies); Branch Catalogs; Interlibrary Loan (note that DVDs are a type of movie format, but many patrons would call them DVDs rather than "movies" or "films")

Oops! We seem to have duplications here: Library and Main Library; Type of Branch and Library Branches. A little discussion is in order. *Note:* It's better to have more potential objects and to do the mental work to determine whether they are the same or different rather than miss a library object.

In the grouping that includes My Library Account, Library Card = Login?, and Library Book Renewal, we might have a duplication; we need to discuss whether a book renewal is the same as a library card. Online, we'd log into our account to view activities, including our book renewal information.

Here's something straightforward: Magazines/Periodicals have Articles and so do Newspapers. A patron would look for an article, but the object itself belongs to the larger objects. In fact, these library objects are called *containers* because they contain little library objects that can be represented by themselves (you could look for an article in a library) but generally are accessed through a larger object. Think about opening a magazine to get an article; that's what you conceptually do when you search for an article. Databases are tools to help you do this rather than being ends to themselves. The magazine is a container. The article is the object.[1]

Hmmm, it appears as though Library Events has a (subset) Read to Me Schedule (story times for kids). Community Calendar Information and Community Events Information might be similar.

Note that Teenager Corner and Kid's Corner stand by themselves, although each has many of the other library objects as a part of it. Maybe they are tiny little libraries within Main Library, similar to branches or special services . . . or maybe they are a type of separate library. Think of these as special content areas with content appropriate to age groups.

Continue to narrow by characteristics as well as to regroup into larger logical sets of library objects that make sense to patrons until you feel you are right. The point is that the grouping should make some kind of innate sense to patrons. In other words, whatever is grouped together has a common idea behind it. Do not worry about whether patrons can identify or articulate what constitutes a group. We organize and act on patterns all the time in our environment without being aware of the concepts behind them.

Meanwhile, we've regrouped all the potential library objects from the original table into logical groupings. The result appears in figure 7-3.

Note: We realized that while Library Card is a library object, it really doesn't exist without a patron-owner (implied, but fits our "has a" rule from earlier). So we changed Library Card = Login? to My Library Account to ensure that patrons understand that it's their own personal account. Also, we decided that the following potential library objects had Services in common; that is, they all fit the "library services are :" rule we discussed in the "What comprises a library object?" section of this chapter: Library Book Renewal, Books on Wheels (bookmobile), Email, Help, Interlibrary Loan, Internet Availability, Read to Me Schedule (story times for kids), Research, Reserves, Services for the Blind, and Study Guides.

We found a new item when looking at the grouping that contains Community Events Information and Endowment, Annual Foundation Appeal—we realized that many of the library objects would fit on a community calendar or bulletin board and that our library should have one; it would make conceptual sense to patrons and allow us to place many library objects logically in one place. It's quite efficient, too.

One object that we originally put in the Services category in figure 7-3 was Library Book Renewal. Then we realized that this would be on our library card screen and we'd view it there, but it really was a task, not a library object.

 Public Library Objects Groupings	
Library Objects	**Groupings**
"Circulation"	Articles, DVDs, Books, Interlibrary Loan
Books	Bibliographies, Books on Wheels (bookmobile), Interlibrary Loan, Special Reading Lists (summer, best-sellers), Pathfinders, Library (Book?) Renewal (this is action, not item), Journals, Magazines/ Periodicals, Read to Me Schedule, Reference, Subject Index, Circulation
Services—some are Events really; place there instead	Books on Wheels (bookmobile), Email, Interlibrary Loan, Internet Availability, Help, Library Item (Book?) Renewal (this is action, not item), Pathfinders, Read to Me Schedule (story times for kids), Research, Services for the Blind
Community (new item)—Meetings, Events, both library and community events	Community Events Information, Community Calendar Information, Endowment, Annual Foundation Appeal, Information about the Community (college, city, etc.), Library Events, Read to Me Schedule, Calendar (new item)
Card Catalog	Branch Catalogs (library has, not card catalog), Databases, Help, Special Reading Lists (summer, best-sellers), Journals, Books, Articles, Newspapers, Magazines/Periodicals, Subject Index and all library items previously under Circulation: DVDs, Interlibrary Loan, Pathfinders
Library News and Events	Community Events Information, Community Calendar Information, Endowment, Annual Foundation Appeal, Board of Directors, Jobs, Staff List
Library	Library Branches, Library Events, Type of Branch, Branch catalogs, Help, Endowment, Annual Foundation Appeal, Kid's Corner, Teenager Corner, Library Magazines/Periodicals, Books, Special Reading Lists (summer, best-sellers), Reserves, Reference, Café, Internet Café, Board of Directors, Email
Internet	Email, Internet Availability, Internet Collections or Links
Patron (new item)	My Library Account, Library Card = Login?

FIGURE 7-3

Object Groupings for a Public Library

We moved it off this listing after making sure that we'd listed it as a task (see chapter 6). That makes sense, doesn't it? See how much you understand? Let's move on.

Okay, this is manageable, isn't it?

Redesign Reflection: Take a look at your current home page now. Can you imagine how overwhelming it might be to a new visitor? How many library objects or pieces of them are shown? What kind of regrouping might help?

Patrons object—or do they?

Some of you may be saying right now, "Are you suggesting we place library objects on these pages and design the elibrary around library objects?" If you really said that, you may breeze through the next section and then jump ahead to chapter 9. For the rest of the mere mortals like us, please proceed to this little step: we're going to select library objects by patron group, continuing with the public library example.

Once again, we are going to determine how important the library objects are to targeted patrons and how frequently patrons use these objects. Remember the patron groups in chapter 5? They include college students as well as a reader and a community meeting room user. We'll put them into our next table and decide which of those groups would use the library objects listed earlier in figure 7-3. We'll list the library objects we have and decide how important each one is to these targeted patron groups or how frequently each is used, again narrowing after much discussion about how often something is used (based on tasks we've gathered).

All right, we're going to do some magic and pretend we just had this discussion, which you can imagine for yourself. We've decided that the items in figure 7-4 are major (important, frequently used) library objects.

This is really a set of building materials for your home page; it's where you can start to see what elements will comprise your site.

Library Objects and Patron Groups				
Library Objects	Patron Group			
	Adult Patron	*Comm. Member*	*College Student*	*"Reader"*
Card Catalog	X		X	X
Books	X			
Services		X		
Community News and Events	X	X		
Library	X			
Internet	X			

FIGURE 7-4
Final Library Objects for a Public Library

How are these objects represented on our site?

In redesigning, we don't want to see all these library objects in full detail all at once on a web page. There's not enough space. An alternative, abbreviated representation of a library object easily recognized by a patron will be sufficient. Computer folks call these depictions or alternative representations *views*.[2]

Every library object has multiple views—it can be represented at least six different ways on a web page. This sounds difficult to understand, but bear with us—this is very, very easy to understand. Don't try too hard.

Let's consider a very basic item, a book. Here are some ways that a book can be represented visually: as a picture of a book with a title on it; as a picture of an open book; on a shelf with its spine showing the title along with other books. Electronically, a book, such as *Gone with the Wind,* can be represented as a title, as a hypertext link, and as a bibliographic record. And if you are a programmer, you also realize that a book can be represented with a control called a list box, which is similar to showing a bunch of spines on a shelf. These are all *views* of a book.

This isn't so bad, is it? There are all kinds of views to a library object. Here's a synopsis of the most common types of view a library object can have:

> as text
>
> graphically, or as an icon or picture
>
> as a textual hyperlink
>
> in a list (also called *list view*)
>
> in an area like a page, with all its details
> (*page view* or *detail view*)

What is a detail view?

Let's look more closely at detail views. Detail views of library objects are where you will place all the information about an item and, generally, that item only. An example is the detailed view of the meetings and events calendar from the Harrington Public Library in chapter 9 (fig. 9-4).

Note that you can place views of other library objects nearby so that patrons can get them; however, the detail view shows only information about that specific library object. When you are looking at information about a book, for example, the major portion of the page will show that information only, or at least the information won't be mixed up with information about other books. In another example, Search Results, the major portion of the page will show the

Search Results, not a lot of other stuff that doesn't have anything to do with Search Results.

Why is that important? In non-Web real life, when you open up your (paper) monthly calendar to view it, you wouldn't expect to see a telephone directory as part of the calendar. This avoids "conceptual confusion."[3] So for now, let's keep this simple.

What do we do with all these library objects?

Why do we care about these views? Because after we determine which library objects are major library objects, we are always going to make sure that when patrons need them, they are always evident and available.[4] Why? (Remember that grocery store example?)

First, patrons won't get lost. They'll always know what item they are using. In the library, the patron will think, "I am reading a computer magazine."

Second, patrons will be able to get around without help because they'll be navigating by looking only for the library object. "I want an article. . . . It belongs in a magazine. . . . I am seeking the magazines. . . . I will open the magazine and find the article. . . ."

This is what people mean when they talk about *intuitive patron interfaces*—there's a gut-level feeling that (1) the environment makes sense, and (2) it's familiar, nonthreatening, and okay to do further exploration. *Sense*, of course, means a familiar pattern or structure underlies the web site, whether or not patrons are consciously aware of it.

This simple example is obvious, but the complex end of the spectrum would be, "I am looking at a list of available books coming to me in the bookmobile."

What's next?

Congratulations—you have completed the analysis phase.

Chapter 8 discusses determining how much to redesign a site or when a complete design from the beginning is necessary. It also brings back "design implications" and introduces advanced discussion about usability and how it's implemented through design. It's an optional chapter, and you might want to glance through it.

Chapter 9 starts the design phase of our process. In this chapter, you take the pieces garnered through the analysis phase and lay out your design.

Chapter 10 discusses the basics of how to evaluate your new design.

Chapter 7 checklist

- What library objects exist in your library?
- How are your library objects represented?
- Which library objects are intruding on other library objects and need to be reassembled?
- Which library objects are most important to your targeted patron list?
- Which library objects might be confusing to your targeted patron list?

NOTES

1. For more about containers, see Microsoft Press pp. 20–21.
2. Object-oriented user interface design shouldn't be confused with object-oriented programming, although the two areas have been drawing closer to each other in the past few years. The authors suggest avoiding confusion among technical and non-technical team members by clarifying this at the beginning of your redesign.
3. There is a wealth of material about interface design and object task modeling available in the software development world. What we are discussing in this book derives from IBM's OVID methodology, which may be of great interest to technical implementers of web sites. (see Roberts et al). Van Harmelen (see bibliography) presents a thorough discussion of the subject from the user interface viewpoint.
4. See IBM's Ease of Use site for more about visibility of objects.

DESIGN OR REDESIGN?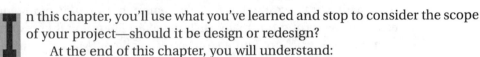

8

In this chapter, you'll use what you've learned and stop to consider the scope of your project—should it be design or redesign?

At the end of this chapter, you will understand:

- the difference between design and redesign
- what to do if you can't redesign right now and want to just fix your site up a bit
- what to fix up
- how to redesign for usability (principles of usability and design)
- how to use design implications for design or redesign

If you're confident you want to get to the process, skip the first two parts of this chapter and read chapter 9, "The Process of Redesigning," for the actual steps. You should, however, read the last section of this chapter, "Design Implications Revisited," because it's part of the process.

What is the difference between design and redesign?

At some point you'll need to decide what to do with your initial site. This decision point may come before you begin to make changes, after your site goals have been determined, after assessing your new design (either by evaluations during the iterations or by the feedback you've received), or after receiving patron feedback after you've launched your changes.

Usability experts may make this type of decision based on factors like the following: which pieces in the analysis need to be changed (which indicates the severity of the usability problems); where in the process changes can be made (which tells us how complicated the site will be to fix); and how much effort it will take to make the changes.

With your knowledge of the process and the pieces needed for object-based design, you probably now know: Will you have to do a little more work by changing the interaction paths but keeping your initial basic design? If you can rearrange pages and reorganize a few library objects or object views, there won't be a lot of changes.

If you can't redesign, can you just fix it up a bit? You may be wondering when a fix up becomes a redesign. The following section will help you decide what comprises a redesign for your site.

How do we know what to fix up?

Start with what's wrong. Decide as a team what's *really* wrong and what's *perceived* to be wrong but really isn't an issue. Then you'll know what to fix, the scope of the problem, and also when to fix what. Maybe your site has experienced some of these symptoms:

> Patrons, higher-ups, or other important people tell
> you that it looks out of date.
>
> Patrons complain that they can't easily find things.
>
> Patrons leave the site quickly without even trying.

What kind of feedback are you getting from patrons? Perhaps you've done some testing or collected data in other ways, and you have a list of problems that patrons have brought up. Go through the list and reorganize it, keeping in mind the following questions: Do patrons say that they are getting lost or can't find things? Are they the patron groups you've targeted? If so, then you need to focus on those patrons and tasks. If they are not targeted patrons, then what are the implications about their perceptions?

If you're not certain how important the patrons' statements are, compare them to the design implications for that group and determine how closely you have matched the patrons' requirements. For example, is a site for novices easy to use or does it include too much advanced information up front, producing "fire hose fear"?

Next, what kind of feedback are you getting from higher-ups? Which concerns are important, now and in the future? Many times, cosmetic issues are brought up; these types of fixes are rarely helpful and, in fact, are a hindrance to an improved site, if they are a substitution for actual redesign.

Redesign decision checklist

The following questions should give you some idea about where the redesign may have strayed. They are listed in order of severity, ranging from easy to difficult to change. Use your goals statement to verify your findings.

Patrons: Are patron groups clearly defined? Are they undefined, not clearly defined, or in groups that are either too broad or too narrow? Are you focusing on patron groups that are not targeted? Have new patron groups become important to the library but their tasks and goals have not yet been accommodated within the design?

Vision or conceptual model: Does the site have conceptual models? Whose are they? The librarians'? The system programmer's? Or the patrons'? Do you need to rearrange or edit existing conceptual models?

Library objects: Are patrons getting lost navigating the site? Can they find library objects and views of library objects? Are library objects—or object details—mixed together? Are the library objects they are finding the same library objects that they use in their tasks? *Redesign Tip:* If your library objects are nearly perfect, see the following section, "Easy Fixes," for more about what to do.

Tasks: If patron groups are correctly defined, are you clear on all the tasks by patron groups? The most severe problem arises when the tasks cannot be accomplished easily using the current interface. That generally indicates that a redesign, starting with an analysis, is necessary. Are the tasks correct but you need to reorganize by object or patch up the object views? If the tasks are correct, is the task-related terminology used by the library confusing to patrons?

Note that we're not asking about your site goals here; if feedback from patrons or others implies that you are not meeting their needs, then most likely your site goals are not congruent with patrons' perceived needs. Compare the two and decide what changes you need to make.

Easy fixes

There are easy fixes for any site. The reason we don't list them first here is to reinforce this notion clearly—be careful. You may spend time and effort on something that will aggravate patrons expecting minor miracles (especially easier ways to do tasks). This can really cause public relations problems with patrons.

That said, here are some easy fixes with pros and cons noted:

Graphical changes: Sometimes a site gets a "redesign" so that the graphics are more modern or up-to-date. Be really careful with this one; it raises patrons' expectations, and it is just a new coat of paint. If someone is pushing for a redesign that only changes the look of the site, review your goals plan and pick some low-hanging fruit at the same time. (*Note:* We are so cautious of this type of improvement that we refer to it as lipsticked livestock.)

Language changes: Review and clarify the site's use of terminology to make sure patrons know what you're talking about. It's been said a million times, but we'll say it one more time—avoid jargon if possible (language particular to a profession). *Keyword* doesn't mean much to most nonlibrarians; we all know how it's confused with *index*. OPAC is just another meaningless acronym to a patron. The only caveat here is that you have to stay in balance with all patron groups so the site language is neither too dumbed down nor too obtuse.

Library object rearranging: Review library objects and object views to see if you have library objects or mixed pieces of library objects, or if pieces of other library objects are intruding into your library objects. Reassemble your library objects as much as you can, make as many major library objects as you can visible from everywhere, and try walkthroughs of taskflows to see if they've improved.

Help documentation: Add some object-oriented help, FAQs, or a site map. The authors are divided on the subject of site maps; one feels that they are necessary, but the other feels that they are often symptomatic of poor site organization, although extremely helpful when the site is not easily navigated. Remember, lots of patrons don't use help, FAQs, or site maps.

When do we redesign?

Most teams don't have the resources to launch a brand-new site that is completely redesigned in one big effort. And most redesigns are complex enough that you have more work than resources. This is not uncommon. Phase the fixing through iteration and scheduled changes.

First, start with your resources. Both authors have worked on web and library sites that needed complete rebuilds, and in all cases this was not quickly accomplished, but patrons appreciate the fixes even when they come more slowly. It's also a good way to keep you on track and organized rather than taking a scattershot approach.

Second, use the old standard—multiple iterations—to slowly and incrementally make changes. Patrons will appreciate it, especially if you have involved them through evaluations or planning.

Read the redesign example for a special collections library later in this chapter to see what a phased redesign looks like.

Redesigning for usability—principles of usability and design

We mentioned design and usability in chapter 2. A redesign should generally be less complex appearing than the original design. The good news is that you will most likely be redesigning the site to appear more simple and easy to use. The goal of design is to achieve unity, which is simplicity (but not dumbing down).

Here are three principles to keep in mind throughout the process of redesigning: unity, intuitiveness, usability.

Unity principle

You've been learning all along to group and regroup. This provides *unity,* a type of congruence or internal set of rules that underlies the entire design so that it makes sense—it "works" for anyone who views it or uses it. Unity is an underlying principle that allows us to do all kinds of abstract things, like thinking, more easily. It allows us to go into unfamiliar environments and be able to navigate through them without having to devote much of our brain to exactly, consciously, *how* we are able to navigate. When an environment (like a web environment, in this case) takes little effort to understand (we "get it" right away or at least pretty quickly, and we feel comfortable making new choices based on what we think will happen), then we are in an environment that by this definition can be called *intuitive*. It makes sense because it has unity; you might also think of it this way: the conceptual model is complete and is reinforced visually as well as behaviorally.

Intuitiveness principle

An intuitive environment provides to users the most basic principle of usability—ability to navigate the environment and to make navigation decisions without assistance. When you understand your environment, you can make completely new decisions, based on the underlying principles, or unity, of the design. That's because you can extend the environment and make accurate guesses about what would be logical, based on the fact that at some level, which probably isn't a conscious level, you understand what can and can't be done next. (Speaking a language is exactly like this. You know how to speak it but probably can't explain it. Even so, you can construct any kind of sentence possible without knowing exactly how.)

User-friendly principle

These completely new decisions that you can make include, within a web site, decisions to "go" and "do" whatever you like. When the site has been designed for intuitiveness, that's what happens. Users enter and leave without meeting obstacles like losing their way. They find things where they should be. And when they leave the site, they feel confident that the experience was not unpleasant. If they need or want to come back, they will, because they remember enough about the site to use it without a lot of effort and, of course, with less hesitation than if the site made them feel stupid, lost, or frustrated. This is the definition of a *user-friendly* site.

Design implications revisited

We talked a bit about design implications at the end of chapter 5 when we looked at the targeted list of patrons for the special collections library.

Design implications are developed by considering the characteristics of each patron group. For every type of patron, certain considerations in preparing the site design will apply. One easy example of a design implication is this: because older patrons may have deteriorated eyesight, the font size on the site might need to be larger than for other, younger patrons who typically would be able to read smaller print.

EXAMPLES

Design Implications for the Special Collections Library

Let's return to the special collections library patron groups (see fig. 8-1). First, we looked at how many characteristics were shared by patrons and whether a high or low percentage was really important. For example "Frequency of site use" showed up as "infrequent" in nine out of our ten initial patron groups. (Remember, at this time we were looking at all groups before narrowing, considering the long-term design implications and how to rank redesign work after we decided

Characteristics by Patron Group (Ten Initial Groups)		
Characteristic	**% Groups**	**Patron Groups—Notes**
Frequency of site use: infrequent	90	Everyone but the academic patron group uses the site infrequently.
Information versus knowledge desired	80	Eight of our original ten groups were seeking information.
"Fire hose fear"	70	Seven were afraid of "too much, too fast."
Subject knowledge: low–medium	60	Over half of our originally defined groups are not subject experts.
Data reliability (content)	60	Six short- and long-term targeted groups wanted quality data.
Author's search for self	50	Of the five, four were important groups looking for this.
Data reliability (bibliographic)	50	Five short- and long-term targeted groups expected reliability.
Content—extent available	50	Five short- and long-term targeted groups expected abstracts and full text.
Interface attractiveness	40	Students and two funder groups were attracted by visual appeal.
High motivation	40	Four groups would be using this site no matter how good or bad.
Power—control	30	Three important groups had high needs for control and power.
Computer comfort level: low–medium	20	Two important groups were not comfortable using computers.
Web savvy: low–medium	20	Two important groups were not comfortable using the Web.

FIGURE 8-1
Patrons and Characteristics

on a phased redesign schedule—that's why we had ten groups totaling 100 percent.) Academic researchers were the only patron group that used the library frequently. Does that information signal anything to us? It doesn't mean that we should split everyone into two groups, the frequent versus the infrequent users.

We also noted that "Web savvy = low" occurred for only two patron groups, but these two groups are very important to the health and well-being of our library, so this characteristic becomes important to remember.

Now we have *two* important patron groups whose characteristics we need to consider: infrequent patrons and patrons with low web savvy.

Design or Redesign?

Going through how often the characteristic occurs (say, six of ten groups have this characteristic) and discussing the relative importance of each finding, we ranked all of the characteristics and their importance by patron group by assigning various weights to user groups.

After we decided which characteristics were most important, we considered how these might be translated along with everything we now know into design implications. From this information, we made the following observations and decisions about our redesign.

Frequency of site use: Nine out of ten patron groups are infrequent visitors to the site. Researchers are the only frequent visitors. This means that all other groups may have problems remembering how to use the site, particularly the advanced features. This library needs to look familiar and friendly every time they visit. We need to provide something like wizards or a My Site page so patrons can easily meet their goals without having to relearn how to use the site.

"Fire hose fear": Seven out of ten patron groups would fit this description. A large portion of patron groups are afraid of this kind of library site! To them, it's too academic and presents too many choices (see our green bar menu in fig. 8-3 for a screen shot of the original site design). Also, we know that too much information too soon will discourage patrons from proceeding or even returning. We will need to use progressive disclosure.

Site attractiveness: The library site traditionally has been quite functional looking; this interface has always been considered adequate for researchers. Note that interface attractiveness was rated as an important factor for four out of ten patron groups, all of whom are important to us either now or possibly in the future. We need to make this site more attractive. (We decided that the look should be modern and weblike.)

Computer comfort and web savvy: Both the funder and architect patron groups scored low to medium on these parameters. *Note:* There are only two groups, but notice that they are targeted patron groups. Their weight counts here. We need to make this site very easy to use. (We also decided that the spell checker had to be fabulous and made this a long-term objective for site improvement on the programming level.)

Subject knowledge: This was an interesting find. Subject knowledge was low to medium for six out of ten of our patron groups. While this is a content issue, it can also be approached in terms of design. Patrons will not be familiar with turfgrass subject headings, which means (1) in terms of site interface design, we must hide them from the patrons, and (2) there will be a heavy load on the thesaurus, which should be considered by the librarians who categorize the site content.

Power and control: A psychological factor quite specific to patron groups using this site was the need for power and control. Three out of ten targeted patron groups would find this a factor in their use of and satisfaction with the site. We all agreed as a team that to ignore this would significantly affect our design and our library goals list.

Content issues: On the bonus side of all this work, information we have collected about library content issues will help the library staff make decisions about acquisitions in the future. Regarding information versus knowledge desired, eight out of ten patron groups want information (casual), not in-depth knowledge. Of the patron groups, six out of ten will be concerned about data reliability in content. Ego involvement (e.g., author search for self) would be important for five out of ten patron groups. Half of the patron groups will be looking for their own name. Because they are a large percentage of our current or targeted population, this becomes an important factor in terms of the content of the site. Obviously, authors must be easy to find! Half (five out of ten) of the patron groups were looking for bibliographic data reliability. Regarding content (extent available), again half of the patron groups (five out of ten) would be looking for this.

Motivation: Another area not linked to our design was high motivation (to use the site). Four out of ten patron groups would most likely continue their tasks even if the site presented problems to their ability to accomplish this. Most likely the other patron groups would quit more quickly if their search yielded zero or unacceptable results. We noted that the search engine must be very good, which again includes spell checking.

EXAMPLE

Redesign in a Special Collections Library

Here's an example of designing using information gathered. The special collections library had a green bar page with a plethora of search options (see fig. 8-2, p. 86). After looking over our patron groups and the design implications noted in the preceding example, we realized academic researchers would know about searching by parameters, but our other patron groups were confused by all the choices.

Because we knew that our patrons would be more comfortable with gradual improvements, over a two-year period we slowly modified this page to that shown in figure 8-3 on p. 86.

We continue to make small but important incremental changes to the site over time, according to the plan we've developed and based on the patron groups information we initially collected as well as more information we continue to collect.

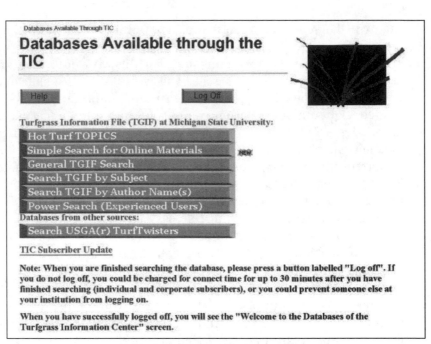

FIGURE 8-2
TIC Original Home Page

FIGURE 8-3
TIC Redesigned Home Page

Design or Redesign?

What's next?

Chapter 9 starts the design phase of our process. In this chapter, you take the pieces garnered through the analysis phase and lay out your design.

Chapter 10 discusses the basics of how to evaluate your new design.

Chapter 8 checklist

- What is design versus redesign?
- Are you going to redesign or fix?
- If you are fixing, what will you specifically fix?
- Which principles of usability and design does your site need to incorporate?
- Which design implications will affect your design or redesign?

THE PROCESS OF REDESIGNING

As promised, the process is what determines the type of design we are presenting—in other words, you've already done most of the work. Now you'll literally assemble the pieces from chapters 4 through 7 into web pages (see fig. 9-1). A description of the process is given along with examples, but to finish your design you'll be building it yourself—and you won't need much additional direction from us. Congratulations—you're nearly there!

At the end of this chapter, you will understand:

- the steps in redesigning
- why this method makes navigation on your elibrary web site flexible and usable

PHASES and TASKS			
Set Site Goals	**Analyze Site**	**Redesign Site**	**Evaluate Site**
Review Mission and Vision	Define Patrons, Tasks, and Library Objects	**Design Using Patrons and Tasks**	Evaluate Site with Patrons

FIGURE 9-1
Redesign Process Chart—Redesigning

What are the steps in redesigning?

Step 1: Establish your objectives

Remember the discussion about design in chapter 3? The goal of design is to achieve unity, which is based on simplicity. We're going to keep narrowing everything again, but this time we'll finish with the simplest redesign we can make that accommodates everything important to our site's success.

We'll base it on what we have now collected in chapters 4 through 7. Using the public library again as our example, we have the following items:

> Goals statement from our library
>
> List of targeted patrons
>
> Goals of these patrons (what they come to the library to do)
>
> Tasks (specific steps patrons must do to accomplish their goals)
>
> Library objects used by targeted patrons

So, let's begin. Let's start with our goal. We've just collected many library objects used by patrons. Like all good designers, we want to try for the most simple but thorough design we can make. That means we'll be going through several iterations of the design to determine the balance between too much and too little as well as checking to make sure that our navigation works.

There's room for only the most important, or major, library objects on the home page of the library. *So our objective will be:* place the minimum amount of library objects we can on the home page and throughout the rest of the site without losing any patrons as they navigate within the site and perform their tasks.

Step 2: Design the home page

First, we're going to place the library objects that are most commonly used or are most important for major patron groups' tasks on the home page—and by now you know which library objects those are in your library! Patrons will basically "walk through" the library objects—they'll select a library object, open it up to work with its characteristics, and, when they're done with the library object, go on to access other library objects. This is the true interaction of the design—and the beauty of it—because you haven't had to second-guess exactly how or in what order patrons are doing tasks.

Don't worry about the exact placement of the library objects at this moment. We are designing from the user behavior perspective rather than for aesthetics now. An artistic team member or a graphic designer can finish the actual look of the web pages after you've determined the design underpinnings.

Public Library Proposed Home Page

Figure 9-2 shows an example of this step, based on what we've learned about our public library analysis. We started with a simple mock-up.

Teen link

Harrington Public Library
4592 West Truman Street
Harrington, IL 60602
224-555-1212
harringtonpl@harrington.org
About the Library

Kid link

Lincoln Branch
721 Lincoln
Harrington, IL 60602

Downtown Branch
7869 Main Street
Harrington, IL 60602

Events & Meetings | Catalog | Services | Internet Links | My Library Account | Help Desk

Try our new email reference service!

Voter & Election Information

Community Links

New Items at the Library

Renew Books

Volunteers

Employment

Contact Us

Site Map

Photo of the library

Last updated 9/1/02   © 2002 Harrington Public Library

FIGURE 9-2
Public Library Home Page—Word Version

The Process of Redesigning

We are really halfway to a redesign. We think this page will support the following major patron group sample tasks, which we've determined are frequent, important, or both:

> Adult researcher wants to ask a reference question
>
> Adult community member wants to reserve a meeting room at the library
>
> Adult patron wants to renew books
>
> Adult community member wants tax information
>
> Kid wishes to know what time story hour is on Saturday and what is the story

Step 3: Do a walk-through?

From your own listing of scenarios, pick a patron group and one task for a walk-through. This is where you will determine if you've got an action that a patron will do for every corresponding step (subtask) you've got in your detailed tasks. Choose an easy one first. We're going to walk you through Marie's task from chapter 6. Marie would like to reserve a community meeting room for her New Garden Books group.

She goes to the library, looks over the available rooms and dates, signs up for a room, and posts a notice on the bulletin board for the meeting.

Marie's task comprises the following subtasks:

> look for available room
>
> look for available date
>
> sign up for room and date
>
> supply contact information for room and date
>
> receive confirmation about room and date
>
> post a notice about meeting
>
> receive confirmation for the notice

Marie enters the elibrary, shown in figure 9-3, p. 92, where she can see several items in the library. *Note:* The items she's seeing are those library objects that we tentatively assembled in sketch one of our home page (see fig. 9-2, p. 90).

In a real library, Marie would walk over to the community bulletin board, which has a calendar. In the elibrary, Marie will select the Events & Meetings hyperlink and open it up to view its details.

Perhaps she'd view the page shown in figure 9-4, p. 92.

Marie opens the Reserve a Room Online link and finds the following information, all about meeting rooms—and *only* about meeting rooms: a policy

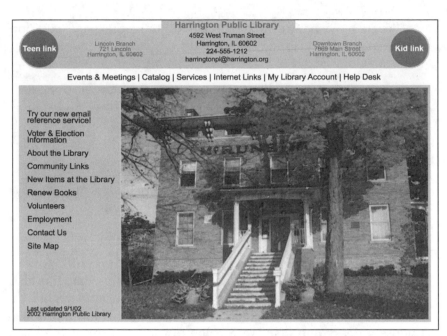

FIGURE 9-3
Public Library Home Page—Web Version

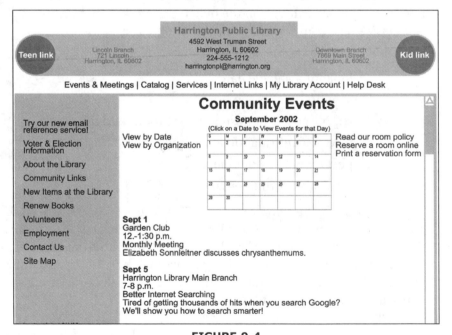

FIGURE 9-4
Public Library Community Events Page

The Process of Redesigning

statement about the use of the meeting room; a registration area with details about the meeting, date, and contact information; and a reservation form to print or email.

Now, while Marie is doing this, it's almost as if she's in a room but is able to look around and see the rest of the library. (Computer magic—the conceptual model!) At any time, Marie can still "see" the areas and items shown in figure 9-5. Not easy to get lost, perhaps.

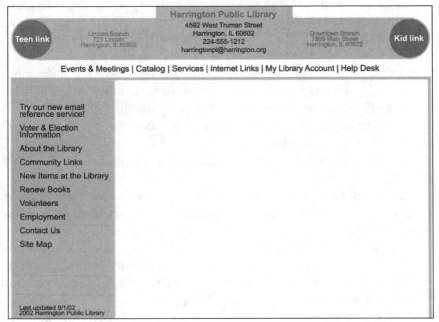

FIGURE 9-5
Public Library Top and Side Navigation

Here's a crucial design point: because we are designing by using common library objects, patron groups share library objects. They have library objects in common, but the tasks that they do may be totally separate. It doesn't matter. The tasks may change, but the library objects won't change. We now can try a walk-through for all tasks that share this library object to see if it works for every targeted patron group. We know they have library objects in common from our work in chapter 7 when we decided which library objects were important or frequently used. A kid might view Events & Meetings to get story hour information (or she might visit the Kid link, where there would be some type of Events & Meetings view also).

The Process of Redesigning

Probably the best example of a library object in common would be the "virtual reference librarian," which we call Help Desk and "Try our new email reference service!" on this home page. Think about all the questions a librarian might be asked. It doesn't really matter to the librarian working the reference desk what the question is. She's a kind of "collection of answers" for the task of "ask a question about something." Millie asks a reference question about Egypt. Marie wants to know how to use a form to reserve a community room. The same situation exists for the items in the library. Think about how much more elegant it is to place one library object on the page rather than list all the possible reasons someone might need to use the library object *and* keep the list current.

Note that we've used two views, or links, to the same detail page to reinforce the characteristics of two types of users: advanced users, who would generally look for the Help Desk, and new or novice users, who would more cautiously look around for something familiar and find "Try our new email reference service!" which is more literal, definitely a task rather than a library object, and a bit more friendly. *Note:* These multiple paths to a library object occur as part of design life, and we recognize trade-offs as reality. We also are quite sure that this won't confuse patrons as much as accommodate two groups.

You may have noticed that "Try our new email reference service!" is also a task, not a library object. We've also placed My Library Account and Renew Books, another set of identical library object/tasks, together. Some patrons (probably frequent or web-savvy ones) would understand the library object, whereas others (maybe new or novice, maybe task oriented) would look for renewing. Hoover's law of 50-50-90 applies here: one of our former colleagues says that when you have two choices in designing and neither seems the clear choice, there will be a 90 percent chance that half the people will prefer one way and half the other way (and you'll hear about it).

Although we focus in this process on library objects and their views, we also recognize that there are other links that need to go on your web site that are not necessarily library objects. These two exceptions are: frequently used links and links to market your library. Frequently used links may be tasks or library objects, such as "renew library materials" or tax forms from January through April or voter's guides in the fall. The library may also want to use links to market new services, such as virtual reference, or promote a list of new materials.

Sometimes you will be asked to make a link for purely political reasons. It may be a link to the mayor's audio greeting or the college president's picture. It's always smart to be politically expedient. Try to move it into the detail under community events or make the case that the president already has a page in the higher-level college pages, but if your solutions are rebuffed, be prepared to compromise your design just a little in order to keep your own support. Your library director can help you determine whether this needs to be done.

We just looked at library objects that patrons have in common. Now let's look at another reason why we like library objects as the major building blocks of our design—a library object can have many tasks associated with it. By making the library object our focus, and the tasks that can be performed on the library object secondary, not only can we perform multiple tasks with that library object, but also in the future we can just add tasks to the library object and not have to change very much of the design.

Let's look at library card as a good example. What tasks can patrons do with a library card? Here are some:

> Get a library card (register online for a library card)
>
> Fill out the form, agree to library legal statement, and send form
>
> Renew a library card
>
> Get a special kind of library card (talking-book accreditation, visitor's card)
>
> View the history of items taken out on a library card
>
> Print the history of items taken out
>
> Renew items on the library card

Now, what if another, new task comes up involving a library card, for example, "pay your overdue fines with a credit card"? The site doesn't have to be changed to accommodate the task.

Here's where flexibility enters this kind of design. Because it's not task oriented, you don't have to change the design. If we'd designed the page with hyperlinks for all the tasks just listed (for example, Get a library card, Renew a library card, etc.) instead of My Library Account (a library object), we'd have to add yet another task like "pay overdue fine." Trying to find a place on the page for new tasks could get ugly quickly.

What is our definition of *successful navigation* going to be? It's easy! Our major items must always be visible from all areas of the library so that patrons can navigate successfully. Some kind of view must always be there.[1]

Working through the design for the first time

Now, the long process of making certain that the design is usable starts. Try the new design with taskflows and see how well it works. You must try this for every patron and task that is defined as important or frequent. As previously mentioned, if you don't do this yourself, then your patrons will do it for you; they'll let you know exactly where your design does not accurately mirror their taskflows.

We're going to walk through an example and see how our redesigning works.

"Ask a Reference Question"

Millie is going to ask a question using email and a web form. She is looking for a place on the library web site where she can ask a reference question. She's looking first for an FAQ to see if her answer is there.

The authors disagree whether site maps and FAQs should be standard objects on a library's web site. The usability expert says a well-designed web site shouldn't require a site map because it should be obviously navigable without one. Similarly, there's no need to provide FAQs about the site because the information should be easy to find.

The librarian, on the other hand, thinks every web site should have a site map to be a table of contents and to help out when the site's language doesn't work for the user. FAQs may be a quicker way for some users to find the answers to their questions. The experts disagree, so you can't make a wrong decision!

Millie goes to the virtual reference desk and engages with the desk by clicking on the hyperlink "Try our new email reference service!" and opening up what you now know will be a virtual reference desk detail view.

Among the items within the reference detail view, Millie finds a reference email form to fill out and send (see fig. 9-6). She wonders if the virtual reference desk is staffed and whether her questions will just go into cyberspace, never to return answered. If there isn't any information about how often questions are reviewed and answered, she writes her reference question in the blank form and includes the date by which she needs the answer and how best to reach her.

Millie sends her question. She expects either an answer or a clarification from the librarian (in which case she will "loop back," just like in real life, until she gets an answer).

All right, that's "Ask a Reference Question," and it appears as though patrons will be able to perform this task without any difficulty that you can control. Remember, tedious as it can be, for every patron group and its tasks, you need to walk through the design and see if the patron group could successfully accomplish those tasks. Success in this case means being able to do each of the steps within the process without failing because a step is missing. If any part of this walk-through doesn't work, think back through the process to see what is not working; very often just one step is missing. Other problems might include a missing detail about a library object or a missing control, such as a Send or OK button to verify a patron's action.

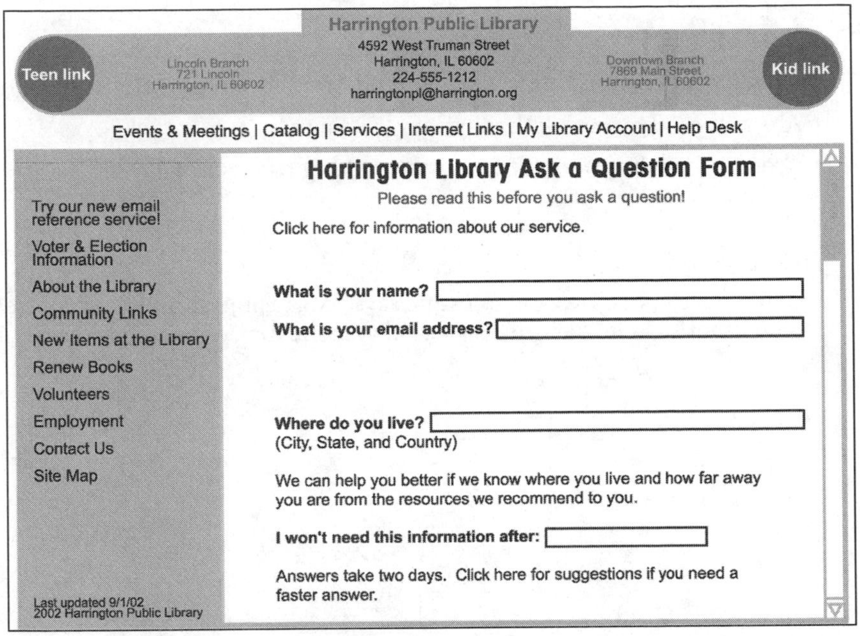

FIGURE 9-6

Web Page with IPL (Internet Public Library) Forms

It's so much easier to do this with the team, making corrections and trying again, than to either (1) take the design to users in a test cycle or (2) receive feedback once the site is open for business and your patrons find these issues for you. Simulate taskflow by patron groups and enjoy this respite between all the analysis work and the actual site redesign launch!

What's next?

Take a break—you've earned it!

When you are certain that your design is good, you need to have people who have not yet seen or used it try the site for you; these people should approximate the patron groups by matching your patron profiles as closely as possible. They'll be trying the tasks that you mapped through the design—in other words, tasks like asking a reference question or reserving a room in the library or placing an item on reserve. Chapter 10 discusses the basics of testing or evaluating your site.

The Process of Redesigning

Chapter 9 checklist

- Have you determined any pieces that are needed for your redesigning?
- Are you ready to work through your design?
- Are you keeping track of fixes and making them now?

NOTE

1. IBM's Ease of Use Design Basics Site says, "Make objects and their controls visible and intuitive," cited at http://www-3.ibm.com/ibm/easy/eou_ext.nsf/Publish/6

EVALUATING AND TESTING

10

This chapter is about determining whether you have achieved your web site goals (see fig. 10-1).

At the end of this chapter, you will understand:

- how to determine if your redesign is successful
- what defines testing and evaluating
- why testing is necessary
- what methods exist for evaluating or testing usability
- the pros and cons of each method
- when to evaluate
- how to evaluate

	PHASES and TASKS		
Set Site Goals	**Analyze Site**	**Redesign Site**	**Evaluate Site**
Review Mission and Vision	Define Patrons, Tasks, and Library Objects	Design Using Patrons and Tasks	**Evaluate Site with Patrons**

FIGURE 10-1
Redesign Process Chart—Evaluation

How do you know you have a good design?

The site might be a good one if your patrons express their satisfaction in any of the following ways:

> Actual compliments (rare!)
>
> Returning to the site often (business picks up)
>
> Phone calls for help asking "how do I do this?"
>
> Others ask how you did it and to give them advice

Actively incorporating usability into your redesign is the very best way to assure that usability is leveraged to its best advantage. The step after that is to try the site out with targeted patron groups and determine how well you've done.

Please note there are many excellent, easy-to-use books about usability evaluations, assessments, and testing, and we recommend them for further reading. We've listed several classics in the bibliography, along with great sources written by librarians about usability testing.

What defines testing and evaluating?

Usability testing is primarily done to determine the extent to which designs reflect targeted user behavior. When we test, we attempt to provide the most naturalistic setting possible. We invite people who match our patron group profiles to perform the typical tasks we've determined to be of importance to our site's success.

What's the difference between a test and an evaluation? Well, a test can be replicated (remember that statistics class?); everything is tightly controlled. Usability testing is very useful in baseline software applications where speed and accuracy—"time on task"—is an issue and users must *quantitatively* improve performance. (One example of a type of test used by usability experts to account for time on task measures how fast and accurately data can be entered into a form.)

Now, that's not very similar to someone searching or browsing a web site, particularly a library web site. We know that some patrons are really thrilled to get a lot of "hits" or results, but just like we know that lots of results don't equal quality data, we realize that other types of quantitative data are not helpful in determining if we're meeting our patrons' goals.

Within an application that relies on *qualitative* measures, such as ease of searching, ability to locate items, and satisfaction with search results, testing is much less important than the effort involved up front in design. For time-on-task testing, the return on investment can be fairly easily determined; that's generally the reason to test. Standard usability best practices show there should be very little "surprise" in testing as well as substantially reduced time and effort to tweak usability performance, if there has been detailed analysis and design.

Use a test if you have to improve a performance standard, such as time to complete a task, or if you need to obtain quantitative information. Otherwise, collect quantitative data through evaluations.

Why test?

First of all, why are you testing? Possible reasons to test include determining return on investment—were the time and other resources expended to improve the site well spent?

In our experience, higher-ups either are committed to usability and usability testing and ready to give dollars for redesign and don't care about return on investment or they aren't. In either case, testing isn't important.

Unfortunately, usability testing is often used for other reasons. It can be political or for publicity value, or perhaps an edict from a higher-up to "do some usability testing" or your grant specifies that you must test.

Testing can be used to reveal design issues and problems, especially when there is little actual information about user behavior. However, testing used this way can spawn a kind of "fix-the-symptom" cycle—you might find yourself focusing on making surface or short-term fixes to the interface based on false or misleading assumptions about patrons, their goals, and so forth and waste time and effort going down an unreal path. What's worse, you may begin to shift your focus to solving problems rather than designing.

Testing can even, goodness gracious, be used as a kind of "marketing vehicle" for patron awareness. We can help you redesign, but we can't make it a better planet; we're trying!

What methods exist for evaluating or testing usability, and when do you use them?

Within the usability process, determining how well goals are met can be accomplished by using walk-throughs, heuristic evaluations, evaluation and testing, or all of these. Here's a synopsis of the *methods* available for determining usability, *how* they are used, and *when* they are most effective in the "usability development cycle."

Evaluating before you design

Up front, during the goals phase, types of evaluations used include heuristic evaluations, comparative analysis, and focus groups.

HEURISTIC EVALUATION

At the beginning of the redesign project, you can save resources by performing, or hiring a usability expert to perform, a heuristic evaluation (also called a heuristic review).

A heuristic evaluation, or heuristic expert review, of the interface design determines the relative severity of typical usability issues (such as navigation, user control and freedom, and error prevention and recovery). Heuristic reviews are very valuable because they allow you to quickly pinpoint issues and balance the amount of redesign effort required for the recommended improvements.

COMPARATIVE ANALYSIS

In a competitive environment, this is used to determine how well others' products are meeting users' needs. For libraries, just check out some similar libraries on the Web to see what they have done that works well.

FOCUS GROUPS

Focus groups are mentioned here because we have very strong opinions about their use and misuse in usability. First, focus groups are great marketing tools, useful for collecting information about what people want or think they want.

As a predictor of patron behavior (which is what we want to evaluate) focus groups provide the kind of data we might get by using a Ouija board. Users cannot generally self-reflect on how they use the library with the kind of detail and accuracy that we can obtain from observation. In a focus group, often the most dominant personalities will take control (this *is* sounding like a séance!), and the insights and thoughtful reflections of less assertive personalities will be lost. Also, focus groups tend to focus, not on users' actual behavior, but on what they think they would like or need. While we might like to give our patrons everything they want, resources limit our ability to do so. Why risk the impression that we can deliver everything patrons might dream up in a focus group while we may know enough about our patrons already through our analysis process? It is far more useful to engage the patrons at the library site itself and collect actual patron behavior as the basis for redesign.

We have seen few focus groups on web site design with successful outcomes and, in fact, do not allow groups of patrons to complete tasks together because of potential difficulties with the compromised behavior that often result when two people attempt to perform the same task. Generally, the more people describe or participate in a task, the less accurate the description will be.

Save the time and energy used on focus groups for strategic design brainstorming.

Evaluating as you design

Here's the rule—during design, test the interface as many times as you can.

During design, a walk-through is generally used. We're going to quote the definition of a collaborative walk-through from the Usability Professionals' Association web site because it's so encompassing:

> Conduct systematic group evaluation of a potential or existing design on a step-by-step basis with a target audience, such as programmers or users, to: identify/validate users' needs; gather design ideas; compare multiple designs; evaluate a proposed design and identify major design problems; identify sources of information to perform tasks; and identity types of processing performed on information.[1]

In general, please, please, please evaluate when you are redesigning and not before. As you have learned, evaluations are primarily used to determine the extent to which interface design mirrors targeted user behavior. The behavior has been previously plotted out and used as a basis for the design.

How do we evaluate?

Here's a short list of the steps in evaluation; please refer to the current literature on usability testing in libraries for details.

1. Set the goals for your evaluation. Metrics to determine how patron success is measured are derived from the goals statement.
2. Decide on the objectives for the evaluation, which include defining how you'll measure patron success in task performance.
3. Make an evaluation plan. It should contain as much information as you can gather about the following:

> Targeted patron groups you will want to use
>
> Tasks that each set of patron groups will perform (mirror the tasks that you've determined are important, frequent, or both)
>
> Templates for evaluators to use
>
> Scripts for evaluators (so that you are as consistent as possible in giving the evaluation and talking with participants during the experience)

Materials used for training evaluators

Forms to gather information about participants

Solicitations for participation

Form letters, including releases

A calendar with time and location

A checklist of materials to bring to the evaluation site

You will need to establish evaluation goals for every patron group. Since statistical validity is not a requirement for this kind of evaluation, most usability folks agree that four to six participants per patron group is a strong enough indicator of whether the site is working well; remember, you may have some no-shows, so plan to add a few extra people.

If you have not done an evaluation before, you may want to seek out someone who has experience to at least walk you through it one time. He or she will be valuable in guiding you through the steps and explaining some of the finer points of evaluating, such as how to treat participants and how to be as uniform as possible during the evaluation, as well as offering other bits of behavioral expertise that will assure you do your best while making participants comfortable and secure about being part of your study.

If you are not able to find an experienced evaluator, remember—you are evaluating the interface, *not* the participant's ability to perform tasks. It's a truism in usability to make certain that participants understand it's a test (or evaluation) of the interface, not of them.

Chapter 10 checklist

- What methods exist for evaluating or testing usability?
- What are the pros and cons of each method?
- Which methods are appropriate for which steps in your cycle?
- What might an evaluation comprise?
- How do we make an evaluation or test?

That's it!

It's time to stick that fork in it and decide if it's done or not. Remember, you can't be perfect when it comes to a web site design, so well done is our goal. One of us had a very funny boss who used to say, "So just put that together and that's it! You're done." Of course, the project involved was always complicated, but he was right; the assembly was lengthy and complicated but not inherently difficult. That's how we feel about this process. We've been through it many times and can tell you this: it's lengthy, there are lots of decisions along the way and many little pieces to track, but assembly is not difficult, it's generally quite interesting, and we're convinced that librarians don't mind this kind of orderly and creative problem solving. Making a flexible design that intelligently incorporates patrons' needs while accommodating change also provides deep satisfaction.

It's our hope and belief that this should make designing or redesigning your web site easier. More importantly, this process should make using your web site easier for your patrons. You should know your patrons intimately by this point. You may find yourself referring to your local donors as Fred or your local garden club members as Marie. That's okay because you got to know them before they became Fred or Marie. Knowing your users puts you light-years ahead of the flashy, trashy web sites that think it's all about cool design. It's all about users.

Usability and libraries both put the needs of the user/patron first, so a pairing of the two fields should prove to be a natural match. Try it and let us know how it goes. The authors are open to your suggestions for improvement. After all—*you're* our users!

Susanna Davidsen
davidsen@umich.edu

Everyl Yankee
eyankee@earthlink.net

NOTE

1. http://web.archive.org/web/20030219130414/http://www.upassoc.org/outreach/common.activities.html

Glossary

404 screen "404 Not Found" is an error message received by World Wide Web users who request a page that is no longer there.

Baseline A standard to which something is compared.

Characteristics Features that distinguish your patrons.

Conceptual model The cultural metaphor with which a person relates in order to accomplish a task, or build or use a web site or a software application. In this book, the conceptual model represents the user's point of view.

Development process A clear plan of how a design or redesign will progress.

Effectiveness How well patrons can achieve a goal.

Efficiency How difficult it is for patrons to achieve a goal.

Flow diagram A flowchart that shows the order of tasks needed to accomplish a goal.

Freedom and control Two seemingly conflicting characteristics that interface users want to have and that make them satisfied with an interface.

Goal statement A statement that describes briefly the goals of a web site.

Heuristics Usability rules of thumb used for a quick evaluation of a software application or World Wide Web interface.

Home page The main page of a web site; the starting point for users.

Intuitiveness An intuitive environment provides to users the most basic principle of usability—ability to navigate the environment and to make navigation decisions without assistance.

Iterations As often and as repeatedly as possible, redesign something and test it immediately with users to determine how well your design is user centered.

Launch The official opening date and time of a web site or a software application to the public or to users.

Learnability How easy it is for patrons to learn how to achieve their goals.

Library objects Anything in a library that patrons will manipulate; everything or everybody in the library with which patrons will interact.

Mission statement   A short, memorable statement clarifying the reasons for the existence of an organization and expressing its purpose and long-term objectives.

Mock-ups   Generally, limited versions of a web site; we mean paper versions in this book. These pages usually have no graphics and use text to indicate links and where graphics are to be placed.

My Site   An application that allows the user to reconfigure the objects and links in a web site to create her or his own home page for the site.

Object-oriented design   Designing interfaces around "objects" rather than tasks.

Patron profiles (User profiles, Personas)   A way of describing your patron groups through one representative person.

Principles of usability   One of the classic definitions of usability says it is measured by "the extent to which a product can be used by specified users to achieve specified goals with effectiveness, efficiency and satisfaction in a specified context of use" (International Standards Organization).

Project timeline   A schedule for a project from start to finish with dates for milestones or events included.

Satisfaction   How comfortable and accepting patrons are with their results.

Scenarios   A set of tasks with only one goal.

Screen shot   A picture of the computer screen.

Subtasks   A set of tasks that make up a workflow.

System centered   An interface that reflects the mind-set of the person who makes it and who is looking at how the computer works from the inside (or system side) out.

Taskflow   The order in which a patron would perform a task.

Tasks   The activities that patrons will perform in order to meet a goal.

Unity   A type of congruence or internal set of rules that underlies a design so it makes sense.

Usability best practices   Standard industry practices for usability professionals.

User centered   An interface that reflects the mind-set of the person who is using it.

User friendly   Users initially comprehend the structure of a web site or remember enough about it when returning so they can use it without a lot of effort.

Views   Alternative, abbreviated representations of a library object.

Vision statement   A statement giving a broad, aspirational image of the future that an organization is aiming to achieve. Vision statements express corporate vision.

Wizards   Software applications that take the user through a task in a step-by-step fashion.

Workflow   A series of tasks to obtain a goal.

Bibliography

Apple Computer Inc. *Macintosh Human Interface Guidelines*. Reading, Mass.: Addison-Wesley, 1992.

Augustine, Susan, and Courtney Greene. "Discovering How Students Search a Library Web Site: A Usability Case Study." *College & Research Libraries* 63, no. 4 (July 2002): 354–66.

Badre, Albert. *Shaping Web Usability: Interaction Design in Context*. Boston: Addison-Wesley, 2002.

Bawa, Joanna, Pat Dorazio, and Lesley Trenner, eds. *The Usability Business: Making the Web Work*. London, New York: Springer, 2001.

Beyer, Hugh, and Karen Holtzblatt. *Contextual Design: Defining Customer-Centered Systems*. San Francisco: Morgan Kaufmann, 1998.

Brinck, Tom, Darren Gergle, and Scott D. Wood. *Usability for the Web: Designing Web Sites That Work*. San Francisco: Morgan Kaufmann, 2002.

Campbell, Nicole, ed. *Usability Assessment of Library-Related Web Sites: Methods and Case Studies*. Chicago: American Library Assn., 2001.

Coad, Peter, and Edward Yourdon. *Object-Oriented Analysis*. Englewood Cliffs, N.J.: Yourdon Press, (Prentice Hall),1990

Collins, Dave. *Designing Object-Oriented User Interfaces*. Redwood City, Calif.: Benjamin Cummings, 1995.

Constantine, Larry L., and Lucy A. D. Lockwood. *Software for Use: A Practical Guide to the Models and Methods of Usage-Centered Design*. New York: ACM Press, 1999.

Dayton, Tom, Al McFarland, and Joseph Kramer. "Bridging User Needs from Object Oriented GUI Prototype via Task Object Design." In *User Interface: Bridging the Gap from Requirements to Analysis,* edited by Larry E. Wood, 15–56. Boca Raton, Fla.: CRC, 1998.

Donnelly, Vanessa. *Designing Easy-to-Use Websites*. Boston: Addison-Wesley, 2001.

Eeles, Pete, and Oliver Sims. *Building Business Objects*. New York: Wiley, 1998.

Elfriede, Dustin, Jeff Rashka, and Douglas McDiarmid. *Quality Web Systems: Performance, Security, and Usability*. Boston: Addison-Wesley, 2002.

Graham, Ian. *A Pattern Language of Web Usability*. Boston: Addison-Wesley, 2003.

Hackos, JoAnn T., and Janice C. Redish. *User and Task Analysis for Interface Design.* New York: Wiley, 1998.

International Standards Organization. "Human-Centred Design Processes for Interactive Systems." *Report ISO 13407:1999.* Geneva, Switzerland: International Standards Organization, 1999.

Krug, Steve. *Don't Make Me Think!: A Common Sense Approach to Web Usability.* Indianapolis, Ind.: New Riders, 2000.

Lauer, David A. *Design Basics.* 2nd ed. New York: Holt, Rinehart and Winston, 1985.

Mandel, Theo. *The Elements of User Interface Design.* New York: Wiley, 1997.

Microsoft Press. *The Windows Interface Guidelines for Software Design.* Redmond, Wash.: Microsoft Press, 1995.

Nielsen, Jakob. *Designing Web Usability.* Indianapolis, Ind.: New Riders, 2000.

Nielsen , Jakob, and Marie Tahir. *Homepage Usability: 50 Websites Deconstructed.* Indianapolis, Ind.: New Riders, 2002.

Norlin, Elaina, and C. M. Winters. *Usability Testing for Library Web Sites: A Hands-On Guide.* Chicago: American Library Assn., 2001.

Norman, Donald. "Cognitive Engineering." In *User Centered System Design: New Perspectives on Human-Computer Interaction,* edited by Donald Norman and Stephen W. Draper, 31–61. Hillsdale, N.J.: Erlbaum, 1986.

Noyes, Janet M., and Malcolm Cook, eds. *Interface Technology: The Leading Edge.* Baldock, Hertfordshire, Eng.; Philadelphia: Research Studies Press, 1999.

Roberts, Dave, et al. *Designing for the User with OVID: Bridging User Interface Design and Software Engineering.* Indianapolis, Ind.: Macmillan Technical, 1998.

Rubin, Jeffery. *Handbook of Usability Testing: How to Plan, Design, and Conduct Effective Tests.* New York: Wiley, 1994.

Schneiderman, Ben. *Designing the User Interface.* 3rd ed. Reading, Mass.: Addison-Wesley, Longman, 1998.

Teorey, Toby J., *Database Modeling and Design: The Fundamental Principles.* 2nd ed. San Francisco: Morgan Kaufman, 1994.

Travis, Tiffini Anne, and Elaina Norlin. "Testing the Competition: Usability of Commercial Information Sites Compared with Academic Library Web Sites." *College & Research Libraries* 63, no. 5 (September 2002): 433–48.

van Harmelen, Mark, ed. *Object Modeling and User Interface Design.* Boston: Addison-Wesley, 2001.

Weinschenk, Susan, Pamela Jamar, and Sarah C. Yeo. *GUI Design Essentials.* New York: Wiley, 1997.

Wood, Larry, ed. *User Interface Design: Bridging the Gap from User Requirements to Design.* Boca Raton, Fla.: CRC Press, 1998.

Xie, Hong. "State Digital Library Usability: Contributing Organizational Factors." *Journal of the American Society for Information Science and Technology* 53, no. 13 (November 2002): 1085–97.

WEB SITES

14 Usability Heuristics from OCLC: http://www.oclc.org/usability/heuristic/set.htm

IBM Ease of Use: http://www.ibm.com/easy

Jakob Nielsen: http://www.useit.com

Jakob Nielsen's Ten Usability Heuristics: http://www.useit.com/papers/heuristic/heuristic_list.html

Macintosh Human Interface Guidelines: http://developer.apple.com/techpubs/mac/HIGuidelines/HIGuidelines-2.html

Susanna Davidsen and Everyl Yankee: http://www.yankeeingenuity.us

Usability Professionals' Association: http://www. upassoc.org

Index

"Millie" (adult learner patron profile), 40
    reference questions, 94, 96
    task analysis, 55–56
mission statement. *See also* Vision statement
    development of, 23–27
    and goals statement, 18–19
    in identifying patron groups, 34–35
Mississippi State University Library (Starkville, Miss.)
    vision statement, 24
mistakes in principles of usability, 12
motivation to use site, 85
multilingual materials not addressed, 5
multiple paths to objects, 94

N

National Freight Transportation Library (Huntington, N.Y.)
    mission statement, 26–27
navigation
    definition, 95
    and library objects, 75
    in redesign decision, 79
    and taskflow, 51, 59
Nielsen, Jakob, 11–12
nonuser patron profile ("Esther"), 40, 61
nonusers of library, 35

O

objectives. *See also* Goals statement
    for evaluation, 103
    in redesign process, 89
object-oriented interface design, 74n2
objects, library. *See* Library objects
observation
    in creating patron profiles, 38
    in determining tasks, 51–52
open-ended design
    and ease of use, 60
    in principles of usability, 12
order of tasks, 58–60. *See also* Taskflow

P

page views, 74
patron behavior, 50–62
patron groups. *See also* Target patron groups
    characteristics of, 19, 42–44
    definition of, 33–38
    identification of, 17, 44–45
    importance of tasks to, 60–61
    and library objects, 73
    in mission and vision statements, 27, 34–35
    patron profiles, 38–41
    in redesign decision, 79
patron satisfaction and usability, 8, 11
personas. *See* Patron groups
physical library
    as conceptual model, 30–31
    mirrored in web site, 12
political considerations
    and infrequent users, 61
    placement of links, 94
    in selection of target groups, 34, 46
    in usability testing, 101
power and control factor, 84–85
processes
    poorly applied, 8–9
    in usability, 8
promises in principles of usability, 12
public library examples
    library objects, 64–72
    mission statements, 26
    patron groups, 35, 37
    patron profiles, 40
    reference questions, 96
    tasks, 53–54, 61–62
    vision statements, 23–24

Q

qualitative measures, 100–101
quantitative measures, 100

R

redesign phase, 16, 17–18
redesign process, 88–98
    complexity of, 13
    definition, 16–18

home page, 89–91
    objectives, 89
    overview, 15–21
    redesign schedule, 48
    redesign *vs.* design, 77–78. *See also* Fixes, easy
reference questions
    sample task analysis, 55–56
    in walk-through, 96
researcher patron profile
    "Mark," 40–41, 66
    "Sandra," 39
resistant patrons and redesign schedule, 21

S

"Sandra" (academic researcher patron profile), 39
scenarios
    in task analysis, 54–55
    in walk-through testing, 91
school projects and research by parents, 67
searching interfaces, not addressed, 5
seasonal information, 61
shopping carts as conceptual model, 30
shortcuts in principles of usability, 12
simplicity in principles of usability, 12, 81
site attractiveness, 84
site maintenance, 8
site maps, 96
special library examples
    design implications, 82–87
    infrequent users, 61
    library objects, 66–67
    mission statement, 26–27
    patron characteristics, 43–44
    patron groups, 36–37
    patron profiles, 40–41
    redesign, 85–86
    redesign schedule, 20
    target groups, 46–47
    vision statement, 24
staff
    in creating patron profiles, 38
    in identifying patron groups, 34

Susanna Davidsen developed the first virtual library on the Internet in 1992. For eight years, she was the director of the Michigan Electronic Library, the state's free online library service. She is now the managing director of the Internet Public Library.

Davidsen was a member of the interface design team at ProQuest and is an adviser and consultant to statewide digital library and portal projects throughout the United States.

She is the associate director for Academic Outreach and Practical Engagement Programs and lecturer in government information, social sciences resources, and business information at the University of Michigan's School of Information.

Everyl Yankee is a usability consultant who has been involved in user interface analysis, design, and evaluation since 1982. She has worked in all phases of development for both software and web-based commercial applications, including ten years' experience with accessible interfaces and extensive experience consulting on e-commerce applications. She was the usability product manager at ProQuest and works with public and university libraries on usability issues.